THE BLESSED WOMAN

A Timeless Journey with Women of the Bible

DEBBIE MORRIS

ACKNOWLEDGEMENTS

Some things should never be attempted alone. I can't imagine writing a book without the support that I have enjoyed. My heart overflows with gratitude to a host of wonderful people. You can't write a book about being blessed without acknowledging the source of all blessings, our Lord. I am grateful that He first loved me.

I want to thank my sweetheart, Robert Morris, for loving me unconditionally. You have represented Christ to me by laying down your life for me. I am blessed and honored to share life with you. Thank you Josh, Hannah, James, Bridgette, Elaine and Ethan. Your love for each other, and pursuit of God reminds me of God's faithfulness. I am so proud of you. Thank you, Grady, Willow and Parker for being you. You are a sweet reward for obeying God.

Thank you, Edra and Grady Hughes for being the best parents a girl could hope for. Your loving support and faithful example chiseled a healthy image of God that provided me an amazing foundation.

Thank you, Jan Greenwood, Lynda Grove, and Mallory Bassham for pushing, pushing and pushing some more. You should take a great deal of credit for the completion of this book. You just wouldn't take no for an answer. I wouldn't want to lead PINK without you. Thank you, Gateway Church Elders for stewarding us well. Thank you, to the Gateway Create team. Thank you, Bobby Williams, Marsia Van Wormer, Mary Zook and Gina Lynnes for carrying this book from a dream to completion. Thank you, Gina, for helping me to express my heart. You were a joy to work with. Thank you, to the Gateway Church for being a wonderful group of people. You put the fun in church.

FOREWORD BY ROBERT MORRIS

I have had the honor of being married to Debbie for the past 31 years. It's been like living with an angel. I honestly believe that if Debbie had lived during Bible times, she would have been one of the women we read about today. Her character, her beauty, her leadership, her love for God … everything about her exemplifies a woman after God's own heart. She's the person who brought me to Christ, and, to this day, she still brings me closer to Him. She really is the person I see the Lord in most.

When Debbie was first asked to speak in front of a group of women, she was reticent and didn't feel as though she had anything to say. Yet, she agreed to do it because she was passionate about helping people know the Lord. The first few times she brought her notes to me to review before a speaking engagement, I was blown away by the things she saw in the Bible. She asked me to coach her in speaking, so I gave her a few pointers, but I felt a bit like Michael Jordan's basketball coach. She was much better than I even imagined! Over the years, Debbie has grown in her ability to see things in the Word that's helping change people's lives. She is an anointed leader and an unbelievable pastor to many, many women … and like Michael Jordan, she's taken off and won the big games.

Many women look for mentors—someone they can emulate. Because of our schedule over the years, Debbie didn't have many in her life, so she chose to learn from women in the Bible. In this book, Debbie shares the applicable truths the Lord has shown her over the years of studying the women in the Bible. Throughout the book, she shares the revelations she has received from these women (and some men!), all while weaving in her own personal story.

Debbie has always had a gift to write, and I am always amazed when I read something she has written. She is a much better writer than I am! This book will minister to every lady who reads it. You'll see yourself in this book. You'll laugh, you'll cry, you'll see truths in Scripture you've never seen before. As you read, you'll see things in your own life that you desire to change, and God's Word will do its work in you because it always has the answer.

I couldn't put this book down once I started, and neither will you! I am so proud of Debbie and so honored to write the foreword for a book containing such powerful principles found in the Word of God. I know as you read and let His truth shine on you, it will literally change your life!

Robert Morris

Senior Pastor
Gateway Church

TABLE OF CONTENTS

CHAPTER 1

LIFE SPRINGS

Adam lay with his wife Eve, and she became pregnant and gave birth to Cain. She said, "With the help of the LORD I have brought forth a man."

GENESIS 4:1, NIV

BEING A WOMAN ISN'T ALWAYS EASY. Most of us discover this early in life. But every once in a while, the full realization dawns on us with especially startling clarity.

For me, the wake-up call came when I was on my way to the hospital about to give birth to my first baby. What an eye-opening trip that was! I'd lumbered to the car feeling calm and competent. Having spent months preparing for the event, I assumed I was ready. Baby showers, doctor's appointments, and chats with other women about the thrills and chills of childbearing had left me feeling supported, informed, and able to navigate the natal experience ahead.

Somewhere between home and the hospital admittance desk, however, my confidence dwindled. Looking down at the rotundity that nine months earlier had been my lap, I wondered if I was really ready for this after all. My heart skipped to a quicker pace as I considered my options.

Clearly, I had none.

There was no way out of this. I couldn't change my mind. I couldn't delegate this task and ask somebody else to finish it for me. I couldn't even procrastinate. *Like it or not, ready or not, I'm going to give birth to this baby today,* I thought. *And I have no idea how to do it!*

Glancing at Robert in the driver's seat, confidently gripping the steering wheel and maneuvering his way through traffic, didn't do much to reassure me. He didn't know any more about this than I did. Yes, he could deliver me to the delivery room, all right. But from that point on, he wasn't going to be much help.

Actually, that's not just a personal observation. It's scriptural as well. As I realized some years later, I was experiencing a little of what Eve did when she gave birth to the very first child ever born. Her description of the event was simple but revealing:

"With the help of the LORD I have brought forth a man" (Genesis 4:1 NIV).

Notice, Eve made no mention of Adam. Apparently, whatever assistance he attempted to give wasn't worth mentioning. (Some things never change.) From Eve's perspective, the only one there who truly made a difference was the Lord. God alone could provide what she needed to meet the challenge of becoming the mother of the entire human race.

Eve's story is so familiar to us that we often take it for granted. But can you really imagine what pregnancy and childbirth must have been like for her? Think of the questions she must have had! Unlike women today, Eve had no example to follow, no mother or sister to explain what was happening to her during those mysterious nine months. She had no books to read about the baby's development, no childbirth classes to prepare her, no friends to share their experiences of labor and delivery.

When Eve's birth pangs began, nurses weren't hovering around her timing her contractions and reassuring her that everything was going fine. She didn't have a midwife to rub her back and put ice chips in her mouth. Doctors weren't tending to her, as they did to me when I delivered my first child, with the efficiency that comes from years of training and experience.

Yet even so, according to the Bible and her own words, Eve was not alone. The all-knowing, all-powerful, all-loving God was there to coach her, comfort her and counsel her. And with His help, she did what she was created to do. She fulfilled the mission that had been divinely woven into her very DNA.

Eve stepped into the calling defined by her name, which means *living* or *enliven*, and brought forth life.

CAN ANYBODY SHOW ME HOW TO DO THIS?

As God's women, we've been following in Eve's footsteps ever since. We've been getting pregnant and giving birth, not only to children but to all kinds of life-generating things—hopes and dreams, ministries and careers, books and businesses. The list could go on and on. But all too often, we've had to walk out the process the same way Eve did: pretty much alone, with only God to help us.

I know what that's like. When I first married Robert and the dream of ministry was conceived in our hearts, I didn't have any mentors—and I needed them badly. As a 19-year-old bride, plagued with insecurities that had nagged me all my life, I had no idea how to nurture and give birth to the plans God had for us.

Our lives back then looked nothing like they do now. Although called to ministry, Robert wasn't even saved when we got married. I didn't know it, of course. I assumed he was! Why wouldn't I? He'd rededicated his life in the Baptist church we attended a number of times. In fact, that's what brought us together. After one such rededication, someone at the church who knew he'd had a problem with drugs suggested he date a "straight girl" to help keep him on the right track. I was elected.

The first time we went out together, we double dated with my sister and her boyfriend. They hadn't yet kissed and he had predetermined that this date would mark the big event. Thus, as soon as the date was over Robert and I quickly disappeared and left them alone.

Slipping around the house to the back door, we started to say our goodbyes when my father appeared, thinking we were vandals or thieves. Donned only in his underwear—yes, the tighty-whitey kind—and as surprised as we were, he said with a dignity that belied his attire, "Deb, it's time to come in."

Mortified, I muttered, "Okay, Daddy," thinking the date was over. Boy, was I wrong! When my father closed the door, Robert kissed me and my whole life changed. Until then, I'd just thought he was cute, nothing more. But that was one great kiss. Afterward, I knew: *This is my guy!* (I realized later the revelation was a great gift from God because it helped me put up with a lot of unexpected stuff I might not have otherwise endured.)

My assumptions about Robert's salvation seemed to be confirmed shortly after we began dating when a local evangelist saw potential in him. He took Robert under his wing and opened doors for him to entertain church youth groups and share his testimony. By the time we got married, Robert was already preaching. There was just one problem: he didn't really know God.

Just nine months after our wedding, our marriage was in trouble and I had no idea what to do to fix it. Robert was miserable. I realize now he was under conviction, but at the time I thought it was my fault. A new bride, eager to please my husband and be a good wife, I wondered in desperation, *What am I doing wrong?*

Thank God, one night after preaching a borrowed sermon based on the parable about the wheat and the tares in Matthew 13, Robert began to realize he wasn't saved and gave his heart to Jesus the next day. Things began to get better because he was rapidly and radically transformed. But even so, life was hard. I faced changes and challenges that left me reeling.

We soon moved to a new city where I had only a couple of friends. Robert traveled all the time in ministry. I went to the young married class at church every Sunday but since I attended alone, I felt like a misfit. Our combined income with both of us working 40-60 hours a week totaled only $600 a month. Although I had no idea we'd ever pastor—and I certainly never entertained the idea that I'd do anything in ministry myself—I knew Robert had a strong call of God on his life. I also sensed that my role, like Eve's, was to help bring it forth.

But how?

Honestly, I had no clue.

Like every woman, I needed a mentor. I wanted someone to walk alongside me, to love me and show me how to get where I needed to go. But I didn't really have anyone. My mother, who is wonderful, wasn't the right person for me to talk to at that point in my life. (Now I have a married daughter of my own, and I understand why that's not always best.) I was working in the offices of James Robison's ministry, and I admired his wife Betty from afar, but I hardly felt like I could pick up the phone and say, "Hi, Betty!

Would you mind being my mentor?"

So I did the only thing I knew to do. I turned to the Bible.

Having memorized Proverbs 31 before I got married, I started asking God to teach me how to be a godly wife. He answered by turning my attention to the women of the Bible. *Of course!* I thought. Ever since my childhood, the characters of the Scriptures have appealed to me. I've never been captivated as much by theology (although I appreciate its value), but I'm fascinated by biblical people and their stories.

As I read and studied about women like Eve, Mary, Sarah, Miriam and Zipporah, the Holy Spirit began talking to me about them. They became like friends and sisters and teachers. Their examples came alive, and the Lord turned them into my mentors. Determined to learn everything I could, to gain all the tips and insights these women had to offer, I found I could grow through their experiences. I discovered, one revelation at a time, what they could teach me about becoming a grace-filled, life-giving woman of God.

You might say they began to give me grace lessons. Lessons I would be learning and living for the rest of my life.

DRAFTED INTO A DREAM

Grace can be defined as *the influence or Spirit of God operating in humans to regenerate or strengthen them.* And I have to say it's the only explanation for what Robert and I see around us today. In many ways, we're living a dream. We're humbled and amazed by the influence God has given us through Gateway Church. Although we've in no way "arrived," we've been blessed to minister to more people than I had ever imagined in those turbulent days when we first married.

Along the way, God has dropped some unexpected dreams in my heart. He's given me a special love for women, for example. He's put within me a deep desire to help them become all He planned for them to be—which is no surprise, really, considering how God feels about His girls. Throughout the Bible, He displays His tenderness toward them. He shows up for them in wonderful and supernatural ways. He's there for them in times of trouble when no one else can help. He reveals Himself to them, speaks to them, and works through them in mighty ways that literally change the world.

I'll be honest, though. When the Lord first started drawing me toward women's ministry, I wasn't exactly an eager volunteer. I felt it was an unrewarding job. As women, we tend to be critical. We have a reputation for picking apart or even undermining what others are doing. We aren't always the best at supporting and building each other up. (You know what I mean. One woman is trying to lose weight and another is saying to her, "Here, have a cookie!")

In women's ministry, when a leader comes with an idea, somebody is likely to say, "We don't want to do that," or "Why don't you do it this way?" I've been reminded of that many times over the years. Shortly after we started Gateway, for instance, I found myself planning a ladies' retreat because another woman presented the idea during our staff Christmas party. We were all celebrating the great results we'd seen that year, munching on sugar cookies and patting each other on the back, when one of the women at the church called me on the carpet. Right there in front of all the other leaders she declared, "We need to have a women's conference!" Then she told me all the reasons why.

Embarrassed and irritated, I grumbled under my breath and muttered, "All right."

For the next few months, I planned the retreat, resenting it the whole time because my heart wasn't in it. After persevering without passion, I managed to pull it off. But guess what? The woman who demanded it didn't even show up. I learned from that experience not to do anything in ministry just because someone else feels like it should be done. If it's not something I'm passionate about, I can't carry it. It's just dead weight. So at least I gained some insight from the fiasco.

I knew such things would happen even before I got involved in women's ministry, so I never intended to sign up for it. But despite my reluctance, God began moving me in that direction years ago at a church where Robert was an associate pastor by drafting me into the small-group ministry there. I use the term *drafted* because one day Robert came home from a staff meeting and announced the decision had been made: all the pastors' wives would begin leading small groups. Although petrified, I wasn't given an option. My notice had been served.

To my amazement and God's credit, my small group expanded and prospered, launching other leaders with their own small groups. Before long, I was asked to join the church staff to help lead our thriving women's small-group ministry. Someone else had seen something in me that I didn't. I was truly honored, but I felt completely unqualified. So for the next several years, I worked tirelessly to hide my own feelings of inadequacy while managing a booming ministry.

When we started Gateway, I was so burned out that I told Robert, "I'm not going to do any women's ministry. Period."

After a few months, however, I relented a little. I started holding occasional social gatherings just to get people from the church together. Then one day Robert came home from a staff meeting and said, "I volunteered you to lead our women's groups."

I'd been drafted *again!* "But I don't want to lead them," I protested.

He paid no attention. "Yes, you know what has to be done. You understand the structure and you've implemented it before in a small-group setting. You have the experience we need."

"Okay," I sighed. "I'll give you six months."

That was more than 12 years ago.

During those years, the Lord has conceived in me a dream of empowering women to follow God with their whole hearts. He's given me a vision of providing younger women with spiritual mothers and mentors who can give them the help I so desperately wanted as a young woman. He's inspired all of us involved in women's ministry at Gateway to encourage and equip seasoned Christian women to become the mentors they are divinely designed to be.

There's nothing new about the concept, of course. It's an idea as old as the Scriptures. Titus 2:4-5 specifically tells us that mature women should teach, train, and encourage "the young women to love their husbands, to love their children, to be sensible, pure, workers at home, kind, being subject to their own husbands, that the word of God may not be dishonored" (NASB).

That's what PINK, our women's ministry, is all about. We're committed to passing along timeless truths, not in old-fashioned ways that resemble a grandmother's tea club, but in ways that relate to today's generation. We've set our sights on celebrating who we are as Christian women and connecting with one another in love. We want to share with each other what we've learned, become cheerleaders for those following in our footsteps, and reach out to receive help and instruction from those who are a few steps ahead.

I will admit, becoming a Titus 2 woman isn't easy for any of us. For one thing, mentoring and being mentored involves exposing our weaknesses. If we're really going to help each other, we have to be honest about our own struggles and pain, and we're not always eager to do that. What's more, investing in other women takes time. Finding a divine mentorship fit requires us to pray over and seek out God-inspired connections.

But, in the end, it's always worth the effort. My friend and associate pastor of PINK, Jan Greenwood, often reminds me of that fact because the first woman who mentored her literally changed her life. "I was like a porcupine when she came along," she says. "I was proud and bossy and really didn't like other women very much. I wonder now how she actually broke through my barriers. But somehow she did—in casual ways mostly, just dropping by to visit or inviting me to take a walk. For two years, by being kind to me and not being religious, she taught me so many things. I didn't know it at the time, but she was mentoring me. Now I look back at that season and realize I was transformed from the inside out by my encounters with her."

DEFINING FEMININITY

All of us who want to be grace-filled women need the kind of encouragement Jan received from that first precious mentor. There are assaults on our femininity from every side. We're living in a day when there are no cookie cutter patterns for us to follow.

We've come of age in revolutionary times when women are making more decisions than ever before. Unlike our mothers and grandmothers, we're buying houses on our own, heading up corporations, and working on cures for cancer. We're fixing dinner, soothing a crying baby, and teleconferencing a board meeting all at the same time. We're wearing hard hats and work gloves so often that hardware companies are designing tools specifically for women.

In many ways, this is a fabulous time to be female. But it's also a complicated time. In fact, without God's guidance, it can get downright confusing.

I was reminded of that a few years ago when I read the book

Love Has a Price Tag by Elizabeth Elliot. In it, she told how she once gave her college students the unusual assignment of defining *femininity* in as few words as possible. Her description of how both male and female students struggled with the challenge intrigued me so much I did the assignment myself.

After searching and searching my heart and mind for an appropriate definition, I finally came up with an answer. Are you ready? Drum roll please.

Because we as women are fashioned wonderfully and uniquely by God, *femininity is living in all the splendor of who God created us to be!*

Which brings us back to Eve.

The original first lady and our first biblical mentor, Eve showed us that as women we are, above all, divinely created to be springs of life: To conceive, carry, bring forth, and nurture that which will enliven the world. God has woven into our DNA the capacity to give birth and to mother—not just physically but spiritually. And as I've discovered both from the Bible and from experience, it's a capacity we never lose.

I delivered my last child 21 years ago, but I've been pregnant every year since. I've carried visions of all kinds and nursed them to maturity. I don't ever plan to stop, either. Giving life is divinely ingrained in me, just as it is in my daughter, Elaine. I saw it surface in her when she was just a toddler. Hardly big enough to walk, barely able to talk, she became a mother nonetheless. She carried around a baby doll everywhere she went—tending to it, fussing over it, and loving it. Nobody taught Elaine to do that. It was just *in* her.

As it is in all of us.

It's a marvelous calling. I wouldn't trade it for anything. But, as I've already said, it isn't easy. The process between conception and birth can be uncomfortable. It often takes longer and is much harder than we expected. Sometimes in the midst of it, we can feel very alone.

That's why I'm writing this book. Because as lonely as we might feel on our way to the metaphorical delivery room carrying within us all the hopes and dreams and visions we've been called to bring to life, we're never really alone. God is there for us just as surely as He was there for Eve. He always shows up for His girls when they need Him most. He loves us in a uniquely gentle way and He knows, as no one else does, how to help us give life—and give it with grace.

As if that's not enough, He's also given us something else: He's given us each other. He's joined us together as believers in the Lord Jesus and made us part of the same spiritual family. He's unified us in the Body of Christ and given us the opportunity as daughters of God to walk and grow alongside each other. To be for one another the spiritual sisters, helpers, and godly girlfriends the first lady in the Garden of Eden never had.

I hope your life is already filled with such women. I pray that you're already surrounded by real-life mentors that meet you for coffee, take life-changing walks with you, or call you on the phone. But if you aren't, there's no need to be discouraged. As I found out so many years ago, God has made provision. He's given us the greatest mentor of all in the Holy Spirit and filled the pages of His Word with women who can teach us a lifetime of grace lessons.

Looking back now, I can see just how far those lessons have taken me. They've introduced me to a life I wouldn't have dreamed possible. I still have much farther to go, but as I continue my journey, I know those wonderful women of the Bible will always be there to help me. I trust as we visit them together through the pages of this book you'll find they help you too.

CHAPTER 2

WHEN GOD INTERRUPTS

Then Mary said, "Behold the maidservant of the Lord! Let it be to me according to your word." And the angel departed from her.

LUKE 1:38

WHEN IT COMES TO THE BASICS of populating the planet, it seems people can pretty much follow their instincts. They don't need a great deal of inspiration to get the job done. Although some information about the process can be helpful, in the literal, physical sense, women often manage to get pregnant without much guidance at all.

Bringing forth life in a divine sense, however, is an entirely different matter. It involves more than following our biological inclinations and letting nature take its course. To conceive and give birth to God-given visions, dreams and callings, we must develop spiritual strength—and a lot of it. We must learn to surrender to the supernatural power of God, override our insecurities, and embrace the impossible by faith.

In other words, we must follow the example of one of the most famous women in the Bible: Mary, the mother of Jesus.

Talk about a grace-filled, life-giving woman! Mary had the privilege of bringing forth the greatest divine dream anyone could ever conceive: The only begotten Son of God, the Savior and Redeemer of the world.

Most of us have heard Mary's story so many times we take it for granted. We sang about it at Christmas time standing on risers dressed as white-robed pre-school choir cherubs. We acted it out in nativity plays at church. We heard over and over again about the angel who came to tell Mary of God's plan and how she responded with a statement so simple and full of faith it's been echoing through the ages ever since:

"Behold the maidservant of the Lord! Let it be to me according to your word."

As children, we didn't grasp the gravity of the statement. To us it was just a line from a Christmas pageant. Even as adults, we sometimes think of it that way. But Mary never did. For her it was a momentous declaration of faith that forever changed her life.

Granted, when she said it, she didn't fully understand the eternal implications. She didn't foresee the magnitude of God's plan of redemption or the honor she'd receive for generations to come because of her part.

No, the day Mary stepped into her divine destiny, she was an ordinary girl living her life much like you and I do on our most ordinary day. She was a typical young woman with normal dreams, preparing to get married, start a family, and live happily ever after. But God interrupted those ordinary dreams and gave her a much bigger vision—a vision that seemed not only unreasonable but downright scary, a vision so intimidating one of the first things the angel said when he showed up to tell her about it was, "Fear not," (Luke 1:30 KJV).

Personally, I'm grateful for those two words. They remind me that Mary was a lot like the rest of us. When she first glimpsed God's great plan for her, her natural response was to draw back in fear. And who could blame her? Just think about what she was hearing!

BEHOLD, YOU WILL CONCEIVE IN YOUR WOMB AND BRING FORTH A SON, AND SHALL CALL HIS NAME JESUS. HE WILL BE GREAT, AND WILL BE CALLED THE SON OF THE HIGHEST; AND THE LORD GOD WILL GIVE HIM THE THRONE OF HIS FATHER DAVID. AND HE WILL REIGN OVER THE HOUSE OF JACOB FOREVER, AND OF HIS KINGDOM THERE WILL BE NO END." THEN MARY SAID TO THE ANGEL, "HOW CAN THIS BE, SINCE I DO NOT KNOW A MAN?" AND THE ANGEL ANSWERED AND SAID TO HER, "THE HOLY SPIRIT WILL COME UPON YOU, AND THE POWER OF THE HIGHEST WILL OVERSHADOW YOU; THEREFORE, ALSO, THAT HOLY ONE WHO IS TO BE BORN WILL BE CALLED THE SON OF GOD." (LUKE 1:31—35)

Even though the angel's message was full of divine promise, Mary's mind must have been staggered by the potential consequences. After all, she knew what happened to unmarried women who mysteriously turned up pregnant in Jewish society. She knew the people of her community would never believe she was carrying a divine child.

As her future flashed through her mind, Mary must have imagined the innuendos and suspicions that would surround her in the years to come. Envisioning the confusion clouding the faces of her friends and family, she must have wondered, *What will they think?* Wincing at the humiliation and hurt her fiancé Joseph would feel, she must have wondered, *What will he do?*

In those first perplexing moments, Mary could have come up with any number of reasons to run from what God was asking of her. She could have cried out, as we're so often tempted to do, "This is too much for me! I can't handle it! I'm afraid!"

But she didn't.

Instead, she dared to believe that God could take a seemingly ordinary girl like herself and do something extraordinary through her. In one of the greatest acts of faith recorded in the Bible, she humbly acknowledged that in herself she was nobody special; then she put her life totally into God's hands, trusting Him to help her become exactly what He said she would be.

WHEN YOU'RE DRAFTED ... LEAN IN

"But that was Mary, the mother of Jesus," you might say. "She was special!"

Yes, she was. But because she was also a real, flesh and blood woman she can be a powerful mentor for us. Because she faced the same kinds of issues and insecurities you and I do, her faith can be our inspiration.

As women, most of us need an example like Mary's to help us believe God can use us in any significant way. We have no trouble believing God can use others but when we look at ourselves all we can see is our inadequacies and inabilities. So, clinging white-knuckled to our comfort zone, we tend to stick with what comes naturally. We shrink back from God's upward call and find ourselves reluctant to say, "Yes, Lord! I'm Your servant. Use me as You please!"

I'll be the first to admit that's often been true of me. I find it easy for me to believe God can use my husband. When we started Gateway, for instance, I had no doubt God would bless it. My excitement soared, and my faith roared into action as I stood on the sidelines cheering God and Robert on!

But when my turn came, I felt altogether different. Faced with leading the women's ministry, excitement fled. Faith faltered. I struggled with the idea of God using me because I know myself too well. I'm familiar with my weaknesses and character flaws. I can see all the reasons why I don't qualify.

When I reminded the Lord of my inadequacies, however, He was unimpressed by them. He drafted me anyway. As I've already mentioned, that's how it felt at first: like I'd been conscripted into a calling I really wasn't fit for. Like I'd been recruited to do something I'd never envisioned I would do.

It's a common experience. Maybe you can relate. Maybe you've felt forced into a career or a marketplace ministry because you have to work for financial reasons. Maybe you felt inducted into motherhood with the unexpected results of a pregnancy test. If so, you know as well as I do that God's plans for us don't always fit our pre-conceived ideas. Rather than being offered as a choice, they often arrive like draft notices and take us in a direction we never expected to go.

Yet, uncomfortable as it may be, God steers us in those directions for our own good. He does it so He can shine on us, in us, and through us into the lives of others. And I've found that by leaning into His plans, we can always find the greatest joy.

Of course, it took me a while to discover that. (In many ways, I'm discovering it still.) Even after reluctantly accepting my call into women's ministry, I initially took it on as only a temporary assign-ment. *I'll fill in the gap until someone more well-suited comes along*, I reasoned, *then I'll quietly resign*. After a few years, that's what I did. I decided my tour of duty was over and stepped back into a more comfortable role at home behind the scenes.

I was happy about it, too! I liked my comfort zone and man-aged to stay there for a year or so. Determined not to meddle in a ministry I'd handed over to another, I tried to stay out of it and mind my own business. But there's something about God's draft notices. As long as you're committed to doing His will, they keep showing up. They follow you wherever you go.

I suppose that's why, as much as I tried to resign from women's ministry, I continued to care about it. So when I noticed it drift-ing from the vision, I decided to mention it to Robert. (Bad idea.) Catching his ear over lunch one day, I pled my case. "Honey, I am concerned. I want to share with the women's team about the direc-tion I think we might be taking, but I don't have the authority to change anything," I told him.

Picking up his cell phone, he flipped open the keyboard and started typing.

"Robert, I'm pouring out my heart here!" I said. "Why aren't you listening to me?"

No answer. Just more typing.

Fairly bristling with indignation, I asked him when he finished to justify the interruption. "So what was so important?" I said.

"I was just making a note to re-instate you as the women's pastor," he replied.

"Whoa, hold on! I'm not even sure I want to do that," I argued. But even as I said it, I knew my argument wouldn't stand. God was drawing me again toward the dream of blessing women, a dream

He has called me to conceive, carry, and deliver. This time, however, I didn't want to do it just because my husband asked. I wanted to receive it by faith as a part of my divine destiny. So instead of resisting, I leaned in. I accepted women's ministry as God's vision for my life and said in my heart, "I belong to You, Lord—spirit, soul and body. Let it be to me as You say."

When I did, something supernatural happened. The favor and blessing of God came upon me to enable me to do what the Lord wanted me to do. I know it not because I felt a special spiritual thrill or because anything unusual happened, but because Proverbs 8:33-35 says:

> HEAR INSTRUCTION AND BE WISE, AND DO NOT DISDAIN IT. BLESSED IS THE MAN WHO LISTENS TO ME, WATCHING DAILY AT MY GATES, WAITING AT THE POSTS OF MY DOORS. FOR WHOEVER FINDS ME FINDS LIFE, AND OBTAINS FAVOR FROM THE LORD.

God's favor always rests on His Word. So when we receive His instructions to us by faith, His favor comes upon us as well. That's what happened to Mary and that's what happened to me. When I embraced God's call on my life, I received the favor and grace to walk it out. Although there was no angel in manifestation to make the announcement, at that moment Luke 1:45 applied to me just as it applied to Mary: "Blessed is she who believed, for there will be a fulfillment of those things which were told her from the Lord."

PROTECTING THE VISION

If believing by itself was enough to bring forth the fullness of divine dreams and destinies, Mary's story could end there. We could appreciate her inspiring statement of faith and look for another mentor to teach us what to do next. We could search for someone else to show us how to take the dreams God has dropped in our heart and carry them until they come to pass.

But, thankfully, Mary's story doesn't stop there. She didn't just make one statement of faith and then lapse back into her normal routine. She didn't casually assume she'd finished her part of God's plan and leave everything else up to Him. Instead, she went into action. She promptly packed her suitcase and left town.

Now Mary arose in those days and went into the hill country with haste, to a city of Judah, and entered the house of Zacharias and greeted Elizabeth (Luke 1: 39—40).

Why did Mary head for Elizabeth's house?

Because she understood something we all need to learn: when God speaks to our hearts about our future and our life's call, we shouldn't run right out and tell everybody about it. That can complicate things. If you doubt it, check out what happened to Joseph in the Old Testament. After blurting out the details of his God-given dreams of leadership, he found himself waiting at the bottom of an empty well while his jealous brothers sold him into slavery.

I hate to break this to you, but our family members and friends aren't always as enthusiastic about our dreams as we are. Sharing everything with them right away can be a mistake. It's wiser to guard what's in our hearts and keep it to ourselves for a while, to shelter and nurture it and allow God to develop it in His own time.

The Bible says Mary "kept ... things and pondered them in her heart" (Luke 2:19). I found out just how crucial such pondering can be when I got pregnant with our second child, James. His birth was unusual because before he was conceived, the Lord said to me, "Have your next baby at home." My first delivery had been a C-

Section, so it sounded risky and I was less than excited about the idea. Rather than reject it outright, however, I said, "Okay, Lord. I'll do it if Robert agrees." I figured that would get me off the hook for sure because Robert would never sign up for a home birth.

After enjoying a couple of smug days thinking I'd safely skirted the issue, Robert and I started talking about our future baby. To my surprise, he was hearing the same direction from the Lord. Aware that some people might wonder about the wisdom of our plan, I decided to keep it relatively private. I guarded myself against negative influences and input. Surrounding myself with godly women of faith who would build me up, I spent time throughout my pregnancy meditating on God's Word and building my faith for a safe and successful delivery.

By the time I went into labor, I was confident we'd heard from God; He was in control, and everything would be all right. It's a good thing, too, because we ran into some potentially serious trouble: At the moment of delivery, I pushed and pushed ... and the baby didn't come. When the crown of his head finally appeared, the bluish color left no doubt something was wrong: the umbilical cord had wrapped around his neck and cut off his oxygen.

Everyone was very concerned, but I felt no fear at all for his safety or mine. The moment James was born, Robert and I just started speaking life over him and praying for him. As we fully expected, he turned pink right before our eyes and all was well. (For the record, I don't recommend having a baby at home unless you know you've heard from the Lord.)

After that experience, I understood in a very personal way how crucial it can be for us to guard our God-given vision.

Apparently Mary understood it too. That's why she went to Elizabeth's house. She was on a mission to protect her divine vision.

Aware of the tenderness of the new life growing inside her, Mary wanted to shield herself from negative influences. Keeping her sacred secret hidden from those who might mock and doubt, she went to see the only person she was certain she could trust.

Mary knew Elizabeth would stand in faith with her because she too had recently received a word from the Lord. Just months before Mary's angelic visitation, an angel had spoken to Elizabeth's husband Zechariah and announced that after years of barrenness, he and Elizabeth were going to have a son in their old age. It sounded impossible. But, miraculously enough, the prophetic word was already in the process of coming to pass. Elizabeth was pregnant.

An ideal mentor and cheerleader, Elizabeth appreciated the magnitude of what Mary was facing. As an old woman wearing maternity clothes and sporting a baby bump, she knew firsthand what it was like to wonder what people might be thinking and whispering behind her back. She identified with Mary in a very personal way.

Although more seasoned and mature, Elizabeth wouldn't peer down her nose at Mary's pregnancy with the perspective of a wizened, old matron. She wouldn't arch a skeptical eyebrow and demand to know what kind of shenanigans Mary had been up to. No, Elizabeth understood the supernatural wonder of the situation. For months, her own belly had been fluttering inside just like Mary's with the miracle of new life. She, too, had embarked on a God-ordained journey. Only a few steps ahead of her young relative on the thrilling road to maternity, she was perfectly equipped to be a vibrant confidante, guide, and friend.

Women like Elizabeth make marvelous mentors. They fill up and give out in ways that nourish themselves and give life to others. Because they're living in a "now" world, they know God, believe

Him, and live faith-filled lives. But, as Elizabeth demonstrated, such women don't have to be finished products to bless us. They can still be in process themselves.

Isn't that encouraging? Aren't you glad to know we don't have to have life all figured out to be a good mentor? We don't have to have 50 years of marriage under our belt, all our kids raised, and a successful career to encourage another woman in her particular stage of life. We just need to be a step or two ahead of her so we can offer a few helpful insights she might not yet have.

KEEP EXPECTING THE IMPOSSIBLE

Once Mary had received and protected the vision, she proceeded to do what every woman who wants to give birth must do: she kept expecting.

In natural terms, that's not exactly rocket science. But spiritually, there's more to it than we might think. When we're pregnant with a divine dream or in the process of bringing forth a supernatural word from God, we must not only keep expecting; we must keep expecting the impossible! We must overrule our limitations and dare to believe day after day: "with God nothing will be impossible" (Luke 1:37).

That doesn't mean we ignore the facts. It doesn't mean we won't have questions when we see the problems involved. Mary certainly did. She knew full well that according to natural law virgins can't get pregnant, so she asked the logical question. "How can this be, since I do not know a man?"

The angel answered by explaining that her child wouldn't be the son of a mere man but the Son of God. He would be the fulfillment of Isaiah's prophecy, "Behold, the virgin shall conceive and bear a son" (Isaiah 7:14) by the power of the Holy Spirit. Therefore, what Mary saw as a limitation (her virginity) was actually a qualification!

The same can be true in our lives as well. The very things we assume would disqualify us from fulfilling God's call are often what qualify us for it. Our human weaknesses and natural limitations give God a perfect opportunity to show Himself strong in us.

I often like to remind myself of this when I'm asked to speak in public because my limitations in that area are excruciatingly obvious. I have no natural aptitude for it. Having always been shy, I took a speech class in high school only because my mother said I might need it someday, which I thought was a ridiculous idea. Needless to say, I didn't take the class seriously and finished it as inept as I began. So when I speak in front of a group and the Lord helps me, He gets all the glory because everybody knows I can't do it on my own.

I'll acknowledge it took me a while to develop that attitude. (In fact, I'm still working on it.) For years, when Robert and I would travel to churches and minister, people would ask me to teach ladies' meetings or lead a Bible study, but I managed to avoid it. Surely, God wouldn't expect that of me, I reasoned. *It would be unreasonable! He knows my limitations.*

One of my favorite cartoons shows a school boy standing toe-to-toe and nose-to-nose with his teacher in front of a blackboard brimming with unfinished math problems. Mouth open wide, his face filled with frustration, the boy is shouting, "I'm not an underachiever! You're an overexpecter!"

Although we sometimes feel like He is, God is not an overexpecter. He knows the greatness of His own power. He knows the amazing things He can accomplish in us and through us. Even though in ourselves we may not have the capacity to achieve what He's asking, He can equip us and empower us to do all things through Christ who strengthens us.

For Him to do so, however, we must drop our negative assumptions. We must stop focusing on impossibilities. God uses people who aren't hindered by what they assume He can't do. Just think about the miracles that happened because:

- Joshua didn't assume the sun could not stand still.
- Elisha didn't assume an iron axe head couldn't float.
- Peter didn't assume he couldn't walk on water.
- Jesus didn't assume the dead could not be raised to life again.

Faith expects the impossible before it happens. Faith believes what it can't yet see. To have the kind of faith that will transform a ruined marriage, bring wayward children back to the Lord, or turn defeat into triumph, we must be confident of victory even when there's absolutely no visible sign of it.

"But Pastor Debbie, I don't have that kind of faith!"

Don't worry. You can get it if you have a Bible because "faith comes by hearing, and hearing by the word of God" (Romans 10:17). For your faith to be effective, however, you must take the words *I can't* out of your vocabulary. They're two of the most destructive words in Christianity. They pose a great danger to the Church because they stop God from using us. They thwart the supernatural in our lives.

It's no wonder the devil likes them so much! It's no wonder he starts notifying people early about all the things they can't do.

Every once in a while, however, somebody misses the devil's memo.

Take Marvin Pipkin, for instance.

A young engineer working at General Electric many years ago, he and some other new hires at the company were instructed by their smirking superiors to figure out a way to frost light bulbs from the inside out. The assignment was meant to be a joke because everyone knew it was impossible. Everyone but Marvin, that is. Too much of a novice in the industry (or too much of an optimist) to know better, he succeeded. He not only frosted the bulbs on the inside, he developed an etching acid that materially strengthened each bulb. No one had told him it couldn't be done, so he did it.

Of course, not everyone who overcomes the *I can't* complex has the same advantage Marvin Pipkin had. Many people start out knowing full well the impossibilities they're facing. Helen Keller, for example, was informed outright she could never escape her prison of pain and weakness. "Oh well," she replied, "there's a lot of living to be found within your limitations, if you don't wear yourself out fighting them." Then she proceeded to accomplish things everyone else assumed were impossible. To those who asked how she did it, she advised, "Face your deficiencies and acknowledge them, but do not let them master you."

Einstein would have agreed with that counsel. Unable to speak until he was four years old and unable to read until he was seven, he refused to allow his apparent "learning disability" discourage him. The same could be said of Beethoven, whose music teacher assessed his ability and announced, "As a composer, he is hopeless." And Thomas Edison, whose teachers said he was "so stupid he could never learn anything." And Walt Disney, who was fired by a newspaper editor because he was "not creative enough!"

Next time you're tempted to let your deficiencies stop you from stepping out in faith, think about those people. Then remind yourself that God is the God of the impossible. He specializes in using both our natural abilities and inabilities in supernatural ways for His glory.

- He parted the Red Sea ... but only after Moses lifted his arm.
- He allowed Peter to walk on the water ... but only after he got out of the boat.
- He favored Mary with conception of His Beloved Son ... but first she had to believe.

WHAT MY BASKETBALL COACH COULDN'T TEACH ME

Before we turn from Mary to visit other mentors, there's one more thing I must mention about her. It's something she did that's not specifically highlighted in Scripture, yet it's too important to overlook: Mary devoted herself completely to the vision she'd been given. She invested herself in it, heart and soul. She kept believing, protecting, and expecting until the vision had been fulfilled.

If we want to be life-giving women, we must learn to do the same. We must develop the devotion that inspires us to whole-heartedly persevere until God's promise comes to pass.

When I was in high school my basketball coach, like most coaches, referred regularly to devotion. She talked about devotion to the sport, to the team, to the Alma Mater, and so on. But do you know what she really taught me about it?

Nothing.

What taught me about devotion was marriage.

Devotion is inspired by love, and marriage is a love relationship. I liked basketball, but I didn't love it. So I'm not a basketball player anymore. I am, however, after more than 31 years, still married to Robert Morris. I'm more devoted to him today than ever ... because I love him.

Love is the motivation behind all true devotion. Therefore, to be devoted to the vision God has put in our heart, we must—first and foremost—love the Source of the vision. We must cultivate and maintain our love relationship with Him. Actually, when we fall head-over-heels in love with the Lord, the vision ceases to be our ultimate goal and we set our hearts instead on our relationship with the Vision-Giver. We become willing to do anything He asks, not for the sake of the vision but for Him.

That's just the way love is. I've discovered in my marriage to Robert that I'll stretch myself beyond my comfort zone to do something he wants me to do, simply because I love him. Although I'm not famous for my cooking skills, if Robert asked me to become a gourmet chef, I'd do my best to give it a go. If he said, "Deb, you could really bless me by devoting yourself to the culinary arts," I'd expect the impossible, sign up for classes and start down the long road to chef-dom.

After my first few lessons, of course, I'd be tempted to quit. And I might give in to the temptation if all I had to keep me hanging in there was my vision of being a chef. I might say, "Forget this! I'm not called to cook. I'm called to order take-out." But because my real goal is to love my husband, I wouldn't say those things. I'd get over myself and go back to cooking class. (Robert, when you read this, please keep in mind, *it's just an illustration!*)

This is a truth we must never forget: love is the sustaining force behind all of our God-ordained destinies and visions and dreams. They're conceived through an intimate love relationship with our Creator. They're sparked within us through a divine romance with our Lord. We expect the impossible because of love. We protect the promises God has given us because of love. We devote ourselves to what we've been divinely called to bring forth and stick with it until the finish—all because of love.

Mary could say, "I belong to You, Lord, spirit, soul and body.

Let it be unto me according to Your Word" because she loved her God. And so can we. Following her beautiful example, we can take the divine deposit God has put in our heart and carry it full term. We can give birth, not to the literal Messiah as she did, but to His character, His promises, and His plans.

It's been more than 2,000 years now since Mary's story was first written, yet she's still known today for the life she carried. By God's grace, may we be known in years to come for the life we carried too.

CHAPTER 3

THE GRACIOUS
ART OF LETTING GO

"I prayed for this child, and the LORD has granted me what I asked of him. So now I give him to the LORD. For his whole life he will be given over to the LORD."

1 SAMUEL 1:27-28 NIV

E MPTY. BLINKING AWAY THE TEARS that threatened to spoil the moment, I looked again at the trailer hitched to the bumper of our car, awaiting the long trip back to Texas. Just two days before, our family had stuffed it full with the happy jumble of clothes, mismatched furniture, towels, linens, and who-knows-what-else that my son, Josh, would need for his new life at college. Now, its mission fulfilled, the vacant trailer baked in the Florida sunshine, as empty as the proverbial nest Robert and I were going home to.

A nest without Josh in it!

Okay, to be honest, we didn't really qualify as empty-nesters.

Our son, James, and daughter, Elaine, still lived with us. And in 13 months, when he finished his studies, Josh would be coming back home too. What's more, with Gateway in its infancy, we were as busy as the parents of a newborn. So this didn't need to be a major trauma.

But I couldn't help it. The thought of everyday life without all my children under one roof hovered over me like a thundercloud. We'd always so enjoyed being together! Although I'd relished every season of my kids' lives, these past few years with them almost grown yet still at home had been especially wonderful. We were having such fun. Now, this whole college thing—which I grudgingly agreed was a good idea—had ruined my party!

Determined not to dampen Josh's excitement, I choked back my tears. I tried not to think about the fact that at 18 years old, he was still my baby; he'd never lived alone. Because the college didn't have dorms, he was moving into an apartment we had located for him online. It was so unsavory that when we arrived and I saw it for the first time, I'd cried out a silent but fervent prayer. "Oh Lord, protect my child!"

Forcing a smile, I hid my misgivings and wrapped my arms around Josh in a hug that would have to last me for months. I could already feel the 1,000-plus miles that separated Orlando from Southlake wedging their way between us. Elaine felt it too, so we made sure not to look at each other. Even a split second of eye contact would trigger an emotional meltdown of uniquely female proportions. So, after waving our final goodbyes to Josh, we slid into the back seat together and stared wordlessly out our individual windows as the car rolled out of the parking lot.

It's a wonder we didn't get cricks in our necks. Because that's how we stayed, mile after mile, our heads turned in opposite directions, watching from behind ocular waterfalls as Florida flew past.

In the front seat, Robert and James bantered guy-style while behind us the vacant trailer rattled along like a child's empty wagon.

In the hotel room that night, Robert congratulated me on my stellar self-control. "You did really great today, honey," he said. "You didn't even cry!"

"What?" I asked, checking his facial expression to see if he was joking. Is it possible he was oblivious to the tempest of tears that had raged three feet from the back of his head for the past six hours?

"Robert!" I said, "I cried all the way to the state line!"

As it turned out, both he and James had indeed been oblivious. After so-longing Josh with a casual, "See ya later," as if they were going to see him again after lunch instead of in a year, they'd gotten on with the business of being men. Doing what needs to be done. Driving. Talking about sports. And assuming the mysterious silence that had engulfed Elaine and me was a sure sign we had fallen asleep!

I understood, though. Although their emotions about Josh's absence hit them later, the guys didn't weep the way Elaine and I did, because they aren't women. God hasn't woven into their DNA our distinctively feminine drive to nurture and hold onto the lives God has entrusted to our care. A drive so strong that sometimes we find it hard to let go, even when we should.

You do realize mothers have that tendency, don't you? We can be tempted to cling too long or too tightly; not just to our children, but to our God-given dreams, destinies, and callings. In our determination to protect and direct them, we can stunt their growth. We can selfishly confine them, like oversized philodendrons squeezed into undersized pots, within the limits of our own desires and expectations.

We don't intend to do damage, of course. As grace-filled women, we want the lives we've brought forth to flourish and grow. We want to give them the freedom to be what God designed them to be. But it's not always easy to relax our maternal grip. Sometimes we need help peeling our possessive little fingers off the people and dreams that are dearest to us. We need another godly woman to show us how to trust the Lord and release our children into His capable hands.

Do you know who's done that for me?

Hannah, the mother of Samuel.

CHANGING FROM THE INSIDE OUT

An inspiring example of a woman who learned the gracious art of letting go, Hannah's biblical story begins this way:

> Now there was a certain man of Ramathaim Zophim, of the mountains of Ephraim, and his name was Elkanah ... And he had two wives: the name of one was Hannah, and the name of the other Peninnah. Peninnah had children, but Hannah had no children. This man went up from his city yearly to worship and sacrifice to the Lord of hosts in Shiloh ... And whenever the time came for Elkanah to make an offering, he would give portions to Peninnah his wife and to all her sons and daughters. But to Hannah he would give a double portion, for he loved Hannah, although the Lord had closed her womb. And her rival also provoked her severely, to make her miserable, because the Lord had closed her womb. So it was, year by year, when she went up to the house of the Lord, that she provoked

HER; THEREFORE SHE WEPT AND DID NOT EAT.

(1 SAMUEL 1:1-7)

Those verses reveal a fact about Hannah most of us can relate to: her dream of having a child came wrapped in a very personal kind of pain. Barren for years, she suffered the cultural shame of childlessness. She endured relentless torment and heartache. Her soul yearning for a child she was powerless to conceive, she adopted a perspective that's common in the early stages of a divine dream. She saw her dream as a path to personal fulfillment, as a way to gain what she wanted and needed for herself.

In other words, Hannah assumed what we all do in our spiritual adolescence: that our dreams are all about us.

When she cried out to God to give her a baby, the void in her own life was her primary focus. And as her prayers remained unanswered—unable to think about anything except her own unfulfilled desire—she slipped into depression. She wept ... and cried ... and on her worst days, even refused to eat.

Ever been there?

Sure you have. Me too.

With the possible exception of the part about refusing to eat (what is it about dreams deferred that makes us crave chocolate?), we all throw ourselves pity parties now and then. Most of the time, we don't even have as good a reason for it as Hannah did. Hers was truly a tragic situation. In her day, a woman's value depended almost exclusively on her ability to produce babies. Barrenness equaled worthlessness. Thus, Hannah's crying and dreaming continued until one day she couldn't take it anymore.

After one too many taunts from perpetually pregnant Peninnah and one too many double-helping meals for which she had no appetite, she marched herself up to the house of the Lord, determined to convince Him to do something about the situation.

> NOW ELI THE PRIEST WAS SITTING ON A CHAIR BY THE DOORPOST OF THE LORD'S TEMPLE. IN BITTERNESS OF SOUL HANNAH WEPT MUCH AND PRAYED TO THE LORD. AND SHE MADE A VOW, SAYING, "O LORD ALMIGHTY, IF YOU WILL ONLY LOOK UPON YOUR SERVANT'S MISERY AND REMEMBER ME, AND NOT FORGET YOUR SERVANT BUT GIVE HER A SON, THEN I WILL GIVE HIM TO THE LORD FOR ALL THE DAYS OF HIS LIFE, AND NO RAZOR WILL EVER BE USED ON HIS HEAD." (VV. 9-11, NIV)

Do you see the shift she made there? As she prayed, Hannah's perspective changed. Rather than focusing only on what she could get *from* God, she began thinking about what she could give to God. She relaxed her selfish grip on her own desire and opened her heart to the plan He had in mind. In other words, she grew up a little.

That's what always happens when we bring forth life God's way. We mature and develop. We begin to look beyond ourselves and what we want to see what God wants. It's a transformational process. As we conceive our children and help them grow, we grow too.

And that growth changes everything.

Hannah proved it. The moment she made her inward shift and took a step toward spiritual maturity, her story took a dramatic turn.

> AS SHE KEPT ON PRAYING TO THE LORD, ELI OBSERVED HER MOUTH. HANNAH WAS PRAYING IN HER HEART, AND HER LIPS WERE MOVING BUT HER VOICE

WAS NOT HEARD. ELI THOUGHT SHE WAS DRUNK
AND SAID TO HER, "HOW LONG WILL YOU KEEP ON
GETTING DRUNK? GET RID OF YOUR WINE." "NOT SO,
MY LORD," HANNAH REPLIED, "I AM A WOMAN WHO
IS DEEPLY TROUBLED. I HAVE NOT BEEN DRINKING
WINE OR BEER; I WAS POURING OUT MY SOUL TO THE
LORD. DO NOT TAKE YOUR SERVANT FOR A WICKED
WOMAN; I HAVE BEEN PRAYING HERE OUT OF MY
GREAT ANGUISH AND GRIEF." ELI ANSWERED, "GO
IN PEACE, AND MAY THE GOD OF ISRAEL GRANT YOU
WHAT YOU HAVE ASKED OF HIM." SHE SAID, "MAY
YOUR SERVANT FIND FAVOR IN YOUR EYES." THEN SHE
WENT HER WAY AND ATE SOMETHING, AND HER FACE
WAS NO LONGER DOWNCAST. (VV. 12-18, NIV)

Notice, God didn't give Hannah her desire until Hannah gave her desire to God. Even though her dream of having a child was good, healthy, and divinely inspired, before it could be fulfilled, it had to be submitted and surrendered to the Lord.

When Hannah made that surrender, she didn't just do it in the fleeting fervor of the moment. Her commitment to God was rock solid. She meant it. After her precious little boy Samuel was born, she kept him at home until he was about three years old. Then she took an emotional journey that made our family's trip from Texas to Florida pale by comparison.

She packed up her toddler's suitcase, took his dimpled hand in hers, and made the 10-mile trek from their home in Ramah to the house of the Lord in Shiloh. When they arrived, she brought him to Eli and said,

AS SURELY AS YOU LIVE, MY LORD, I AM THE WOMAN
WHO STOOD HERE BESIDE YOU PRAYING TO THE
LORD. I PRAYED FOR THIS CHILD, AND THE LORD
HAS GRANTED ME WHAT I ASKED OF HIM. SO NOW I
GIVE HIM TO THE LORD. FOR HIS WHOLE LIFE HE
WILL BE GIVEN OVER TO THE LORD."
(VV. 25-28, NIV)

With those words, Hannah turned; and, after kissing her little boy on the cheek one more time, she went back home ... without him.

Can you imagine how hard that must have been for her? Not just to say goodbye to Samuel, but to entrust him to Eli's care?

According to the Bible, he wasn't famous for being a great father. He had two sons of his own who were rebellious, corrupt, and totally profane. Serving as priests under Eli's supervision, they pilfered the people's sacrifices and even "slept with the women who served at the entrance to the Tent of Meeting" (1 Samuel 2:22, NIV). Yet Eli did nothing to restrain them. Although he scolded them a bit, they didn't heed his words at all.

Hardly the best possible role model for Hannah's little boy, Eli had already demonstrated how disastrous his influence could be.

What a situation! It would be tough enough to leave your three year-old in the hands of a good man. So you have to wonder how Hannah ever summoned the courage to leave her boy with a man like Eli.

There's only one possible explanation: her trust was not in man, but in God. She believed with all her heart God would be faithful to care for and keep her son. Because of that confidence, after a short season of holding Samuel close, Hannah was able to release him to his divine destiny.

What she didn't do, however, was abandon him. She kept on loving him, as grace-filled women always do, influencing him in her own, gentle way even from afar. Sewing a little robe for him every year, she brought it with her when she and Elkanah traveled to Shiloh to worship. And each year, after she draped her handiwork over her son's ever-broadening shoulders, Eli blessed Hannah's husband and said:

> "MAY THE LORD GIVE YOU CHILDREN BY THIS
> WOMAN TO TAKE THE PLACE OF THE ONE SHE PRAYED
> FOR AND GAVE TO THE LORD." THEN THEY WOULD
> GO HOME. AND THE LORD WAS GRACIOUS TO HAN-
> NAH; SHE CONCEIVED AND GAVE BIRTH TO THREE
> SONS AND TWO DAUGHTERS. MEANWHILE, THE BOY
> SAMUEL GREW UP IN THE PRESENCE OF THE LORD.
> (1 SAMUEL 2:20-21, NIV)

Although Hannah may have missed having her firstborn under her roof, her nest was anything but empty. Filled with the rewards of her obedience, her home reverberated with peals of children's laughter and the energetic thunder of growing feet. It overflowed with the answers to Hannah's prayers—five beautiful reminders that no matter how much we give, we can never out-give our God.

"Well, that's all good for Hannah," you might say. "But what about Samuel? How did he turn out?"

He turned out to be one of Israel's greatest priests and prophets. He became a greater blessing to more people than Hannah could have ever envisioned. He also moved back to his home town of Ramah and lived there for the rest of his life.

Think of it. He chose Ramah, not Shiloh.

Apparently, even though Hannah's opportunity to mother Samuel full-time was brief, her influence made a lasting impression. Her short season of nurturing, done God's way in God's time, impacted her little boy more than Eli ever could.

NOSE-BLOWING, POTTY-GOING, AND THE STAGES OF LIFE

Oh, how grateful I've been over the years for Hannah's example! It's encouraged me in so many ways. As a young mother when I realized I couldn't personally protect my children 24/7, Hannah's story helped assure me God was big enough to take care of them all the time. I could trust Him to watch over them when I couldn't. Sending them off to school each day after Robert and I prayed for them and asked God to guard them from evil, I could release them to Him with complete peace of mind.

That's not to say I expected Him to protect them from all negative experiences. God never promised to do that. None of us get to float through our days in a divine biosphere, insulated from the hazards of planet Earth. So my children experienced the normal bumps and bruises that go along with growing up. It's a good thing they did, too.

The rough spots kids encounter and the minor childhood pains they feel help them learn to go to God for themselves when they need help. If they never faced any difficulties, they wouldn't develop the strength to overcome them. They wouldn't grow into the conquerors they were meant to be.

That's why, as parents, we need to seek God for the right balance as we guide our children to maturity. We have to avoid the tendency to be overprotective while still being there to intervene for our kids when they truly need our help. It's a challenge, for sure. But over the years, that's what I tried to do. I trusted the Lord, gave our kids the freedom to grow up, and let them know that if they needed an advocate, they could count on me to be there.

When Josh was punished in elementary school for the misbehavior of his entire class just because the teacher thought "as a pastor's kid he should hold to a higher standard," I got righteously indignant. I didn't object to him being punished along with his classmates for doing something wrong. But I wasn't about to sit quietly by while he was made the scapegoat.

I wanted my kids to do what was right because it was right, not because their father is a pastor. So I did what needed to be done about it. Stepping into the role of the protective, warring mother, I went to set the teacher straight.

Would I do the same thing for Josh now?

Of course not. There comes a time when intervening in such ways is inappropriate. You have to discern the season for nurturing your children. In the beginning, when they're little, you're 100% involved. You're everything to them. You wipe their nose. You take them to the potty. But as they grow up, you start letting them take care of those things. When it comes to nose-blowing and potty-going, you let them handle it. You don't even ask them to report to you about it. Assuming no news is good news, you just take it for granted that all is working well.

Maybe that sounds silly, but it's true nonetheless: every life we bring forth goes through different stages. So we have to learn when to protect and give it our all, and when to release it and give it the freedom to grow according to God's plan. Whether that life is a child, a ministry, a project, a business or some other God-given dream, we must realize there comes a time when we can no longer project our own wishes on it. We must let it take on its own personality and follow its own God-ordained course.

I've been through that process with our women's ministry. When I first stepped back into it at Gateway, I was totally consumed by it. My assistant and I exchanged emails at the strangest hours of the night because at that point the ministry was like a baby. It needed 100% of my attention. It demanded constant care and feeding.

Today, things have changed. I don't send emails at midnight anymore. The ministry has grown. It's on a solid path. The intensity of my involvement has decreased because I have a wonderful team of gifted, anointed women helping me. To poke my nose into everything that's going on and try to control it all would be unhealthy. We're in a different season now.

The stages and seasons of growth are something my husband understands very well. He knows how to initiate an aspect of ministry and then release it when the time is right to someone who's qualified to take it to the next level. He sets that person free to run with the vision, but he does it without abandoning them. He provides support and accountability without being a micromanager.

It's one of the key elements of Gateway's success. We couldn't possibly have grown so quickly if Robert felt compelled to know and control everything that's going on. The different elements of the church—things like our Freedom, Stewardship, and Worship Ministries—couldn't have expanded and matured as they have if he'd held on to them with a tight fist.

What enables him to delegate such vital responsibilities to others with such complete peace of mind? He has something in common with Hannah. He doesn't really depend on people to make sure everything turns out all right. Ultimately, his dependence is on God. He has an exorbitant trust in God.

As a leader myself, I try to follow his example. I endeavor to create an environment of trust and support so those who work for me can develop and grow. I share my values, perspective, and vision; but as soon as they're ready, I let my team members stretch their wings. When Robert and I travel, I tell them, "I'll be gone for a while. You can reach me if you really need me, but don't feel like you have to consult me on every decision. Just pray and follow the leading of the Lord yourself. When I get back, I'll support whatever decision you made. If I have any further thoughts about it, I'll let you know."

My goal is to create the same atmosphere that, as a mother, I tried to provide for my children. I never wanted them to be afraid they'd make a mistake. I wanted them to be secure in the knowledge that if they did their best, I'd back them up. If they got something wrong, instead of criticizing or belittling them, I'd encourage and coach them so they could do better the next time.

At home, at church, in the office, or anyplace else, I've found this principle remains true: If we'll nurture with an open hand, put our confidence in God, the precious lives under our influence will have plenty of room to grow.

DO THAT … DON'T DO THIS

As much as I've learned from Hannah, she's not the only mentor who's taught me the power of a mother's influence and the importance of graciously letting go. There's another woman in the Bible who's instructed me too. Her name is Athaliah, and she's helped me the same way the *DO* and *DON'T* photos in fashion magazines help people who want to sharpen their sense of style.

You've seen those pictures, right? Definitely worth a thousand words, they show rather than tell what's right … and what's wrong.

"DO wear this."

"DON'T wear that."

Do wear the stilettos with the evening dress. *Don't* wear the flip-flops. (Or, do flip-flops go with anything these days? I can't remember.) *Do* wear the denim. *Don't* wear the spandex.

Although most fashion editors are probably unaware of it, it's a method of teaching that originated with the Bible. Seriously. The Scriptures are full of snapshots of people who did things God's way … and people who didn't. Those who got it right … and those who got it wrong.

The Bible's snapshots are captured in story form, of course. They aren't literal photos. But if they were, Hannah's would definitely be topped by the word *DO*.

Athaliah's, on the other hand, would be emblazoned with a big, bold *DON'T!*

Hannah's polar opposite, Athaliah, stands apart as one the most wicked women mentioned in the Bible. Born of the notoriously evil lineage of Israel's king Ahab, her rise to prominence began when her son, Ahaziah, became king of Judah. His tragic reign lasted only a year and ended in his death because:

> HE … WALKED IN THE WAYS OF THE HOUSE OF AHAB,
> FOR HIS MOTHER ADVISED HIM TO DO WICKEDLY.
> THEREFORE HE DID EVIL IN THE SIGHT OF THE
> LORD, LIKE THE HOUSE OF AHAB; FOR THEY WERE
> HIS COUNSELORS AFTER THE DEATH OF HIS FATHER,
> TO HIS DESTRUCTION. (2 CHRONICLES 22:3-4)

I think those are some of the saddest verses in the Bible. It's heartbreaking to think that a mother, driven by her own twisted past, would influence her son in such terrible ways that her counsel would end up killing him. Yet Athaliah did it. And, if that wasn't bad enough, once her son was dead and could no longer serve her selfish ambitions, "she arose and destroyed all the royal heirs of the house of Judah" (2 Chronicles 22:10).

Then she reigned as an ungodly queen until she was overthrown and executed six years later.

I know what you must be thinking. You're wondering what on earth any Christian woman would have in common with Athaliah.

You'd be surprised.

When it comes to family ties, we all started out in the same situation she did. Before we committed our lives to Christ, Satan himself was our spiritual father. Talk about an evil lineage! We had the worst there is.

Granted, now that we're saved we're part of a new spiritual family. God is our Father, and Satan no longer has authority over us. But that doesn't mean he's stopped trying to influence us. He hasn't! He still does everything he can to tempt and deceive us into thinking and acting like we're his children. Using negative influences from our past, he pushes us to perpetuate his evil actions and patterns of thought not only in our own lives, but in the lives of our kids, our employees and others we impact every day.

My parents were some of the best in the whole world, so I figure if this is true of me it's true of everyone: we all come into parenting with a negative past. We all pick up undesirable traits and tendencies from family members, teachers and others as we're growing up. If we're not mindful of those tendencies, we'll inadvertently make the mistake Athaliah did. We'll pass them on to our children. We'll inject the harmful effects of our past into the lives we're bringing forth in the present.

Unlike Athaliah, however, we won't do it in blatant ways. (We're hardly going to build idolatrous altars in the living room.) We'll do it more subtly, through our negative words, attitudes, and habits. Have you ever noticed that our kids always pick up on what we wish they wouldn't? It seems they absorb the negative things so much easier than the positive!

That's something I had to be especially aware of with my daughter, Elaine.

Just a few months before she was born, Robert and I were watching an old episode of *I Love Lucy*. As we laughed at Lucy's antics, a thought suddenly struck me. *What would it be like to raise such a strong-willed, red-headed girl?*

When Elaine arrived, I found out. She challenged me from the time she was an infant. I'd dress her in a cute little outfit and she'd throw a fit until I took it off. I didn't realize what a dangerous precedent I was setting: the mother/daughter clothing battles had begun, and she was already winning at six months old!

Elaine's feisty, fearless personality was the total opposite of mine. Without a shy bone in her body, she was more like her father in every way—not the new, improved, post-salvation version of her father, either, but the unsaved, ornery one.

Her two easy-going, obedient brothers rarely got in trouble at school. But Elaine made up for it. In her first week of kindergarten she not only fought the class bullies (a set of twin boys), she defeated them! Her "prize" was a trip to the principal's office. The same week, she informed her teacher she would be taking over the class. Confident she was competent to do so (after all, she'd been lining up her dolls and teaching them for years), Elaine took great offense when her offer was refused.

I may not have known much about raising a strong-willed, red-headed girl back then, but one thing was crystal clear: I could not make Elaine be like me. If I wanted her to be who she is, the person God created her to be, I couldn't project myself onto her. I couldn't pass along to her my own fears and insecurities. I couldn't tell her to be quiet and stay in the background like I tend to do. She's a natural leader, a born communicator. The old-fashioned religious ideas I grew up with (*i.e. women shouldn't speak in church*) would have utterly frustrated her.

So I knew what I had to do. I had to deal with the wounds in my own soul so I wouldn't end up inflicting them on her. Hurting people hurt people. Healed people heal people. The healthier we are in our soul, the purer our influence will be. So I had to get healthy. I had to deal with the pain from my past to make sure it wouldn't leave the scars on my daughter it had left on me.

No doubt, you feel the same way. You don't want to poison your God-given dreams with the leftovers of your own brokenness. You don't want to pass on yesterday's limitations to the lives you're bringing forth today—to your sons and daughters, the women you mentor, the employees who look to you for guidance. You want to position them to mature unhindered. Giving them godly counsel and empowering them to succeed in every season of life, you want to help them grow!

So take a tip from Athaliah. Look around and check the fruit you're producing in the lives you've been nurturing. Take the time to deal with the pain from your past. And, every once in a while, just for good measure, glance again at the biblical photo of the mentor you *don't* want to be.

CHAPTER 4

NEVER TURN YOUR BACK ON A WOMAN OF GOD

"The Lord's victory over Sisera will be at the hands of a woman."

JUDGES 4:9, NLT

A *AT FIRST GLANCE,* she looks like she belongs in a murder mystery rather than the pages of the Bible: Standing, hammer in hand, over the lifeless body of a man she just nailed to the ground. Announcing without remorse to those who've come looking for him, "Here he is. I killed him!"

Most people would be quick to agree, she doesn't exactly fit the stereotype of a grace-filled woman of God.

But that just goes to show you, there's more to such women than most people think. They aren't, as the old saying goes, just *sugar and spice and everything nice.* They can also be armed and dangerous. They can be as brave as they are beautiful and as strong as they are soft. Although they're life-givers by nature, when it comes to dealing with an evil enemy, godly women can be downright deadly.

That's why Satan has always been afraid of them. He found out a long time ago that just when he thinks he has a woman under control, she can turn the tables on him. She can rise up against him and become a victor instead of a victim. Wreaking destruction on the destroyer, she can set entire generations free.

As one of God's girls myself, I like to imagine that Satan has his own saying about us, one that has nothing to do with sugar and spice. I like to think he says, "Never turn your back on a woman of God."

One thing's for sure: somebody should have said it to Sisera.

Of course, even if they had, he probably wouldn't have listened. The Canaanite military commander of King Jabin's army, Sisera would have scoffed at the idea that a woman could cause him trouble. What woman on earth could stand up against his multitudes of soldiers and iron chariots? The entire nation of Israel had cowered under his oppression for 20 long years. He'd cut off their trade routes, strangled their economy, and brought the nation to its knees. Why should he be afraid of any of God's people—especially the girls?

It's a good question. And it also has a good answer.

As the Bible tells us in Judges 4, the rebellious children of Israel had gotten fed up with Sisera's harassment. They'd repented and "cried out to the LORD," and He had heard them.

Sisera may not have known it, but he had major reason to be afraid. *Very* afraid.

His army didn't stand a chance. His godless grip on Israel was destined to be shattered by a head-on collision with an unchanging spiritual fact: the turning point to every oppression comes when people cry out to God.

That was true for Israel and it's true for people today. Seeking the Lord with a repentant heart and asking Him for help is the first step toward freedom. When we acknowledge we're wrong and we want to change, God always delivers us. He empowers us to overcome even the most enormous challenges. He backs us up with His own supernatural might and enables us to overthrow our oppressor. And for those of us who happen to be women ... well, let's just say God can give a whole new meaning to the phrase *fight like a girl.*

Sisera can verify it. His worst nightmare started with a feisty woman of God named Deborah. An Israelite prophetess, she started the revolt that ended in his demise by sending for a warrior named Barak and relaying to him the word of the Lord:

> GO AND DEPLOY TROOPS AT MOUNT TABOR; TAKE WITH YOU TEN THOUSAND MEN OF THE SONS OF NAPHTALI AND OF THE SONS OF ZEBULUN; AND AGAINST YOU I WILL DEPLOY SISERA, THE COMMANDER OF JABIN'S ARMY, WITH HIS CHARIOTS AND HIS MULTITUDE AT THE RIVER KISHON; AND I WILL DELIVER HIM INTO YOUR HAND ... AND BARAK SAID TO HER, "IF YOU WILL GO WITH ME, THEN I WILL GO; BUT IF YOU WILL NOT GO WITH ME, I WILL NOT GO!" SO SHE SAID, "I WILL SURELY GO WITH YOU; NEVERTHELESS THERE WILL BE NO GLORY FOR YOU IN THE JOURNEY YOU ARE TAKING, FOR THE LORD WILL SELL SISERA INTO THE HAND OF A WOMAN." (VV. 6-9)

As you can see from the last phrase of that passage, Deborah wasn't the only woman Sisera needed to worry about. Another one just as dangerous had been appointed by God to finish what Deborah had started.

Her name was Jael.

She was the woman Sisera turned to for help when Deborah and

Barak's army of 10,000 Israelites rose up against him. It's ironic, but it's true: on the day "the LORD routed his troops and slaughtered all his army with the edge of the sword before Barak" (v. 15), Sisera fled on foot—frantic to save his own skin—straight to Jael's tent.

At the time, Sisera's logic made sense. He figured that because Jael was the wife of a Kenite man who had a treaty with Jabin she'd be likely to provide him a place to hide. And, sure enough, at the outset, it appeared he was right. Coming out of her tent to greet the battle-weary warrior, Jael said exactly what he wanted to hear:

> "TURN ASIDE, MY LORD, TURN ASIDE TO ME; DO NOT
> FEAR." AND WHEN HE HAD TURNED ASIDE WITH
> HER INTO THE TENT, SHE COVERED HIM WITH A
> BLANKET. THEN HE SAID TO HER, "PLEASE GIVE ME
> A LITTLE WATER TO DRINK, FOR I AM THIRSTY." SO
> SHE OPENED A JUG OF MILK, GAVE HIM A DRINK, AND
> COVERED HIM. AND HE SAID TO HER, "STAND AT THE
> DOOR OF THE TENT, AND IF ANY MAN COMES AND IN-
> QUIRES OF YOU, AND SAYS, 'IS THERE ANY MAN HERE?'
> YOU SHALL SAY, 'NO.'" (VV. 18-20)

Jael's hospitable response to Sisera seems odd for someone we've chosen as a mentor, don't you think? I mean, really. What kind of woman opens the door to a tyrant, offers him a snack, and tucks him in for a nap? What kind of woman hides the enemy in private while in public she claims she hasn't seen him and everything's all right?

Women like us, that's who.

We've all done it at one time or another. We've entertained the enemy of our soul and tried to keep it hidden. We've let secret sin slip into our thoughts and attitudes. Suffering on the inside from

Satan's oppression, we've smiled on the outside and pretended nothing is wrong.

It's no surprise, then, that Jael chose to do the same. At least for a while. Until, exercising a woman's prerogative, she decided to change her mind.

The Bible doesn't tell us exactly what prompted the change. Maybe as she watched the sleepy Sisera snoring in her tent, she began to think about his cruelty to the Israelites over the previous 20 years. Maybe she remembered with mounting indignation how he'd attacked and killed them when they were defenseless; how he'd stolen their property, and captured and raped their women. Perhaps she pictured the faces of her Israelite friends and contemplated her family's historic ties to their nation. After all, her husband was a descendent of Moses' father-in-law. The Kenites and the Hebrews had been linked for generations.

Whatever Jael's line of reasoning, it brought her to this conclusion: she owed nothing to the Canaanite named Sisera who had brutalized God's people for so many years. He was no friend of hers. He was her enemy, and he deserved to be defeated. Somebody had to put an end to his ruthless reign.

The question was, *who?*

Barak and his soldiers couldn't do it. If they searched Jael's tent without her husband's permission it would be considered an insult by their Kenite friends. Sheltered from Israel's army, Sisera was safe and cozy. The only way to stop his oppression was for Jael to end it herself.

Truth be told, the same thing is true for you and me. We're the only ones who can extinguish the enemy that's resting in our soul. Only we have the power to get rid of him. Others can come alongside and help but nobody else can do it for us. Ultimately, it's up to us to decide we're done playing hostess to the oppressor, get honest about the trouble he's caused us, and use the Word of God to strike him a deadly blow.

Which is precisely what Jael did.

With one difference, of course. Because her battle was literal, she needed a physical weapon and not just a spiritual one to win it. Glancing around her tent, she spotted just what she needed—her hammer. As a Kenite woman responsible for pitching the household tents, she'd used it countless times to drive tent pegs into the ground. She knew how to yield it with speed and accuracy. Reaching for it, she fixed her eyes on her wicked guest and said to herself, *This is a new day!*

> THEN JAEL, HEBER'S WIFE, TOOK A TENT PEG AND TOOK A HAMMER IN HER HAND, AND WENT SOFTLY TO HIM AND DROVE THE PEG INTO HIS TEMPLE, AND IT WENT DOWN INTO THE GROUND; FOR HE WAS FAST ASLEEP AND WEARY. SO HE DIED. AND THEN, AS BARAK PURSUED SISERA, JAEL CAME OUT TO MEET HIM, AND SAID TO HIM, "COME, I WILL SHOW YOU THE MAN WHOM YOU SEEK." AND WHEN HE WENT INTO HER TENT, THERE LAY SISERA, DEAD WITH THE PEG IN HIS TEMPLE. SO ON THAT DAY GOD SUBDUED JABIN KING OF CANAAN IN THE PRESENCE OF THE CHILDREN OF ISRAEL. (VV. 21-23)

ONE PLUS GOD IS A MAJORITY

When Jael killed the enemy hiding in her tent, she didn't just free herself. She liberated a nation. She emancipated generations. When we follow her example, we do too. Our personal victories over sin and Satan affect our husband, our children, and even our grandchildren. When we conquer the oppressor in our own lives, we embolden other believers to do the same. That's why it's so vital for us to identify the Enemy and put an end to him. When he comes to steal, kill, and destroy, we must be determined to take God's Word and drive him into the ground.

I didn't always know such victory was possible. In fact, for years, I had no idea it was necessary. Growing up in a denomination that pretty much ignored the activities of Satan (and the Holy Spirit too, for that matter), I didn't even realize I had an enemy working against me. I tried to be the best Christian I could. But if you don't recognize you're in a battle, it's pretty tough to win. So I spent the first part of my Christian life losing big time without even knowing it.

That's not to say I was involved in anything especially shocking. Raised to be what you might call a *good girl*, I mostly fell prey to the *good-girl* kinds of sin. Pride, for instance. Not the pride that says, "Look at me, I'm better than everybody else!" but the insecure version that worries and wonders, *"What are people thinking about me? Am I dressed right? Am I following the right protocol? Am I saying the right thing, and making a good impression?"* It's an oppressive form of self-focus that kept me busy varnishing the outside while neglecting what matters most: "the hidden person of the heart" (1 Peter 3:4).

I'd still be bound by that kind of oppression today if I'd never learned to identify the Enemy behind it. But, by the grace of God, I did. I found out from the Bible that Satan is very real and much more active than I'd been taught to believe; and like it or not, I was caught in the middle of a spiritual war.

Granted, when Robert and I first made that discovery, we got a bit carried away with it. Like a lot of Christians when they first learn about spiritual warfare, we saw the Enemy everywhere. The traffic light would turn red when we were in a hurry and we'd rebuke the devil. The dinner rolls burned, and it was Satan's fault.

Honestly, it alarmed me at first to think he had so much power.

He doesn't, of course. I realized that later. As I studied the Scriptures I understood that even though Satan is a formidable enemy in many ways, he is no match for the Holy Spirit who lives within me to empower me and teach me. In the midst of a battle, the Holy Spirit can whisper insight to me. He can bring the Word of God to my remembrance. Arming me with the sword of the Spirit, he can make me like Jael with her hammer and tent peg—a mighty woman of God against a battle-weary foe.

Such revelations greatly encouraged me. *The Holy Spirit removes the devil's advantage!* I thought. *He levels the spiritual battle field.*

It sounded good at the time. But it wasn't quite right. As I learned more about the power of the Word and my Helper, the Holy Spirit, I realized the battlefield isn't level at all. It's tilted mightily to my advantage. Because, through Christ, Satan has already been defeated, my victory is assured. If I'll just stand my ground and use my weapons, the war is already won!

At 5'3 tall, I may be just a little girl, but I can route the devil's army because one plus God is a majority!

Actually, we all need to cultivate that attitude because as women of God, it's our job to kill the enemy of our soul—not just once like Jael did, but again ... and again ... and again. For us, and for all believers, walking in freedom is a process. We keep on gaining it, one victory at a time. Engaged in a perpetual battle with an enemy determined to oppress us, we can never sit down and say we've arrived. We can never rightly claim we've secured all the freedom we're ever going to need.

Instead, we must always be on the lookout. We must continually remember that Satan is a ruthless tyrant, dangerous and persistent. He loves to prey on our defenselessness, our ability to provide, and the sanctity of our homes. We can't afford to entertain him for a moment—even in secret! So when we find ourselves under his influence in some area of our lives, we must cry out to God like the Israelites did. We must seek the Lord and ask Him to show us how the Enemy gained entrance, and what we must do to put a tent peg through his head.

"What if Satan gets to me through somebody else's action?" you might ask. "What if I'm under oppression because I've been victimized by another person who did me wrong?"

Then the first tent peg you'll need is the power of forgiveness, because freedom is not for victims; it's for victors. And the only way to step from victimhood to victory when we've been wounded is by forgiving the person who hurt us.

It may sound hard, but we can do it. The Bible assures us that since God has forgiven us we can forgive others. We may have to put some prayer into it, though. I know that from experience. There was a time in my life when I felt so wronged it seemed impossible for me to forgive. I tried to do it over and over, but within hours (or even minutes) I'd find myself fuming with resentment again.

Mentally replaying the injustice I'd suffered, I'd argue my case in an imaginary courtroom. I'd declare my innocence (for the hundredth time) and present the evidence against those who'd harmed me. With great satisfaction, I'd imagine the whack of the judge's gavel as he rendered his verdict against them: *Guilty!*

Then one day, Jimmy Evans preached a message on forgiveness at Gateway. Describing a similar incident in his life, he shared how God had taught him that by praying for the person who'd wronged him, he could break free from the dislike and unforgiveness he felt toward them. I didn't want to hear that! But I swallowed my irritation and put the principle into practice. Every time I caught myself re-opening the case in my mental courtroom, I prayed.

I'll confess, at first my prayers weren't very nice. I prayed things like, "God, show them their wicked ways and be gentle when You smite them." But over time, my heart changed. My attitude softened. I really began to love the people who'd hurt me. I started wanting them to succeed and prosper, and my prayers reflected it.

That's when I knew I was free.

WHAT'S UNDER THAT BLANKET?

In dealing with the Enemy of our soul, we don't always have the advantage Jael did. She knew full well the evil she was entertaining. She knew who Sisera was and what he was up to before she ever invited him into her tent. He didn't sneak in and hide under a blanket while she was pulling weeds outside. He didn't disguise himself as a vacuum cleaner salesman and convince her he meant no harm.

Satan, however, does that kind of thing all the time. He sneaks into our lives when we aren't paying attention. He slips up on us so subtly we hardly even notice he's there. A master deceiver, he covers himself in lies. He dims the light in our soul so he can oppress us in darkness without being seen.

That's why, in our quest for freedom, we should ask God to do for us what David asked in Psalm 13: "Consider and hear me, O LORD my God; enlighten my eyes, lest I sleep the sleep of death" (v. 3). That's a powerful prayer! I use it often when I'm pressing in my own life for a higher level of liberty. It helps me identify areas where the Enemy has been hiding. It opens the door for the Lord to show me sins I've been blind to so I can repent and obey.

As we've already established, that's where real freedom always starts: with repentance and obedience. I've been to the most dramatic deliverance services you can imagine. I've heard people yell at the devil and watched them toss their cookies into paper bags. But you know what? When those services were over, I walked out thinking, *My God is bigger than that.* He doesn't need those kinds of theatrics to deliver us. All He needs is a sincere heart, crying out to Him for help. All He needs is someone who will ask Him to open their eyes; someone who will do what He shows them to do.

In my own life, the most powerful season of deliverance I have ever experienced came through a simple little book full of soul-searching questions. Designed to challenge believers to examine their lives and get honest with the Lord about hidden sin, it asked things like, "Do you have a problem with lying?" (Then it added, "Be honest.")

Because I earnestly wanted to be free from every oppression of the devil, I took those questions seriously. With the Holy Spirit's help, I began to identify the weaknesses and strongholds of sin in my life. Then, as the book instructed, I asked other believers to pray with me about those things. It was humbling, but James 5:16 says, "Confess your faults one to another, and pray one for another, that ye may be healed" (KJV). So I did it. I opened up the hidden places of my heart that no one else could enter unless I invited them.

It still amazes me how much that simple process changed my life. It brought me to a whole new level of freedom, nailing the Enemy of my soul in myriad of ways.

Does that mean I walked away from it finished and fixed forever? Could I brush my hands together and say, "There, that does it! I'm permanently free!"? Certainly not. Although I made a lot of progress in that season, there are always more battles to fight and more territory to conquer.

I was reminded of it in a fresh way just a couple of years ago. At a time when great things were happening for Robert and me in ministry, a major storm blew up in my personal life: I lost my dad. Our kids hit some rough times. Robert and I were writing a book on marriage, busy with the church, and traveling a lot. Pressures mounted from all sides, and I began to crumble.

Nobody knew it, of course. On the outside, I looked fine. So I had a choice to make. Would I just ignore the resentment and frustrations building inside me? Would I opt to play religious games and stand at the door of my tent waving and smiling at people, pretending that all is well? Or would I seize this crisis, get honest with myself, with God, and with another believer, and use the situation as an opportunity to drive out the Enemy and attain a greater degree of freedom?

I chose the latter. Taking a deep breath, I did what I encourage our staff members and our congregation to do when they're struggling. I walked into our Freedom Pastor's office and asked if she had a few minutes to talk.

Oh, how I hoped she would respond to my emotional outpouring with a shrug, a smile, and a pat on the back. How I wanted her to say, "Nothing to be concerned about! Anybody would feel the same way in your situation."

But she didn't. Instead she said, "I think we need to talk about this some more. Can you come back?"

Uh oh. Not a good sign.

As much as I hated to admit it, I knew she was right. So I went to see her multiple times during the next several months. As we talked, I discovered the storm I'd encountered wasn't really the problem. It just uncovered some areas where I needed to change my perspective. Like a gust of wind whipping away a picnic blanket, it had lifted the covers in my soul and exposed a few more sleeping Siseras.

I hadn't even realized they were there. But once I identified them, nailed them, and made the necessary changes, I stepped into a higher place of strength and freedom. I took new spiritual ground, not just for myself but for the others my life will effect in years to come.

Following in Jael's footsteps, I inflicted one more major headache on the Enemy ... and reminded him just how dangerous God's girls can be.

GOD MEANT IT FOR GOOD

She gave this name to the LORD who spoke to her: "You are the God who sees me."

GENESIS 16:13, NIV

FROM THE PERSPECTIVE of my four-year-old grandson, Grady, the incident qualified as a serious injustice. A crime had been committed against him. He'd suffered an underserved blow (albeit by some very tiny hands), and he wanted something done about it.

Never mind that from a grown-up's point of view, the grievance might seem minor. Although it didn't compare on a world-wide injustice scale to what happened to the employees at Enron or the investors who came out on the short end of the subprime mortgage scandal, to Grady this was important. The principles of equity every toddler understands had been violated: he'd played nicely with his little sister, and she had *not* played nicely with him.

Facing me like a miniature whistleblower testifying before congress, he delivered his terse report. "Gigi, Willow hit me!"

I figured right away that even-tempered Willow hadn't inflicted any real physical harm. At 18 months old she hardly qualified as a prize fighter. But I didn't want to add insult to what Grady clearly perceived as injury. So I suppressed a smile and gave him a chance to assess his condition.

"Are you okay?" I asked, somber.

He pressed his lips together and thought for a moment, checking to see if he could identify some scratch on the outside that might match the wound he felt on the inside. Finding none, he realized he'd emerged from the altercation physically unscathed.

"Yes, I'm okay," he admitted. "But will you tell her not to hit me again?"

"Sure I will," I replied.

Satisfied, Grady returned to play with Willow. His little shoulders no longer sagging under the burden of an un-righted wrong, he'd received the two things he needed: First, the ruler of his little world (which at the time happened to be me) had seen and validated his pain. And second, he'd received the promise of a more just future.

Validation and justice. Important stuff. Not just for Grady but for all of us. Whether we're four or forty, when life treats us unfairly and leaves us hurting we all want someone significant to take note of our suffering. When circumstances dish out to us a bewildering batch of disappointment instead of our just desserts, we want someone to set things straight. We long for a person with power to intervene on our behalf as we cry out, our hearts wounded by betrayal: "I didn't deserve this!"

It's a familiar cry, especially here in America where most of us assume we deserve quite a lot. Maybe it's because we grow up knowing we have an inalienable right to life, liberty and the pursuit of happiness, or maybe it's something else. But whatever the reason, as Americans we tend to expect an exemption from injustice of every kind. Despite ample evidence to the contrary, we awaken every morning sold on the notion that as long as we play nicely with the Willows in our life, they will play nicely with us.

We assume if we're hardworking employees, we won't get laid off. If we're faithful to our husbands, we'll never face divorce. If we're good parents, our children will never rebel. If we do good, we'll receive nothing but good in return. In theory, it's as simple and predictable as 2+2=4.

But, as we've all discovered, theories aren't always correct. Reality isn't first grade math. And in life, things don't always add up the way we expect.

They certainly didn't for Hagar.

ENCOUNTERING THE GOD-WHO-SEES

An Egyptian maidservant in the household of Abraham and Sarah, Hagar found herself caught in circumstances she definitely didn't deserve. As convoluted as a calculus equation, they weren't the simple result of her own choices. They were the product of somebody else's poor judgment.

To put it bluntly: Hagar wound up pregnant with Abraham's baby because Sarah decided it would be a good idea.

Young Hagar must have been shocked by the idea when she first heard about it. Most likely, she hadn't exactly been dreaming of putting the moves on her mistress's husband. He was, after all, 85 at the time. But when Sarah added surrogate motherhood to Hagar's household responsibilities, she didn't have any other option.

What else could she do? She was a servant, not a freelance

contractor. She couldn't exactly resign from her position, polish up her resume and go looking for another job. All she could do was watch with helpless wonder as:

> Sarai said to Abram, "See now, the LORD has restrained me from bearing children. Please, go in to my maid; perhaps I shall obtain children by her." And Abram heeded the voice of Sarai. Then Sarai, Abram's wife, took Hagar her maid, the Egyptian, and gave her to her husband Abram to be his wife … So he went in to Hagar, and she conceived. (GENESIS 16:2-4A)

The storyline sounds more like a script from *Desperate House-wives* than a passage we'd expect to read in the Bible. Even taking into account the cultural differences of their day, with Sarah setting up a tryst between her husband and her maid, and Abraham voicing no objection, we might be tempted to recheck our facts: was this really the couple God chose as the father and mother of faith?

Yes, sure enough, they were. Abraham and Sarah were God's covenant people. They're described, along with other scriptural heroes in Hebrews 11, as those who "won divine approval" (v. 39 AMP). They believed God, left their homeland in obedience to His command, and blazed a trail of faith we still follow today. But they weren't perfect. Their walk with God had some question marks in it. They made mistakes. And one of the biggest mistakes they made involved Hagar.

Bless her heart! She didn't deserve to be pregnant. She hadn't asked to carry the child of a man she didn't love and who wasn't in love with her. But such was her life, and it was totally unfair.

So she reacted like anybody would. Faced day after day with the injustice of her situation, her respect for her mistress began to dwindle. Her manner slipped from courtesy to contempt—which, most of us would agree, is totally understandable. "Give the poor girl a break!" we might say. "Get her some counseling. She just needs to work through her feelings!"

Sarah, however, didn't see it that way. She was infuriated. Determined to put Hagar in her place, she poured out her anger to Abraham. Blaming him for the debacle, she said:

"IT'S ALL YOUR FAULT. FOR NOW THIS SERVANT GIRL OF MINE DESPISES ME, THOUGH I MYSELF GAVE HER THE PRIVILEGE OF BEING YOUR WIFE. MAY THE LORD JUDGE YOU FOR DOING THIS TO ME!" "YOU HAVE MY PERMISSION TO PUNISH THE GIRL AS YOU SEE FIT," ABRAM REPLIED. SO SARAI BEAT HER AND SHE RAN AWAY. (VV. 5-6 TLB)

Hagar ran away. It doesn't sound like a very big deal—unless, of course, we consider the obvious question: Where did she run?

Not to the unwed mother's home, because there wasn't one. Not to the church on the corner, because there wasn't one of those either. Abraham and Sarah lived in Canaan, in the middle of nowhere, surrounded by wilderness. So, bruised and pregnant, that's where Hagar went. To wander alone amid serpents and scorpions, searching for shade in the skin-scorching sun. To huddle at night listening to the snarls of the jackals, wondering if morning would find her alive.

Such an end would be bad enough for someone who deserved it. But Hagar didn't. Used and abused, she'd done nothing wrong. She deserved vindication, not a trek through a wasteland. She deserved justice, not a jail made of scrub brush and sand.

Yet there she was. All by herself in the desert. Aching to cry out for help but keeping silent because no one could hear.

And even if they did, they wouldn't care.

At least that's what Hagar thought until she made the most startling discovery of her life: Someone had come looking for her. Someone who not only loved her, but had the power to make her future turn out right.

> NOW THE ANGEL OF THE LORD FOUND HER BY
> A SPRING OF WATER IN THE WILDERNESS, BY THE
> SPRING ON THE WAY TO SHUR. AND HE SAID,
> "HAGAR, SARAI'S MAID, WHERE HAVE YOU COME
> FROM, AND WHERE ARE YOU GOING?" SHE SAID, "I
> AM FLEEING FROM THE PRESENCE OF MY MISTRESS
> SARAI." THE ANGEL OF THE LORD SAID TO HER,
> "RETURN TO YOUR MISTRESS, AND SUBMIT YOUR-
> SELF UNDER HER HAND." THEN THE ANGEL OF THE
> LORD SAID TO HER, "I WILL MULTIPLY YOUR DE-
> SCENDANTS EXCEEDINGLY, SO THAT THEY SHALL NOT
> BE COUNTED FOR MULTITUDE ... BEHOLD, YOU ARE
> WITH CHILD, AND YOU SHALL BEAR A SON. YOU SHALL
> CALL HIS NAME ISHMAEL, BECAUSE THE LORD HAS
> HEARD YOUR AFFLICTION." THEN SHE CALLED THE
> NAME OF THE LORD WHO SPOKE TO HER, YOU-
> ARE-THE-GOD-WHO-SEES. **(GENESIS 16:7-13)**

A WORLD-ROCKING REVELATION

The-God-Who-Sees. What a wonderful name for the Lord! We don't often use it these days but maybe we should. We desperately need the revelation it carries. Especially when we're faced with some crushing disappointment, we need to know God sees our pain. We need to sense He's there with us to hear and answer our hearts' cry.

It's astounding how much difference that can make.

For Hagar, it changed everything. Her encounter with the God-Who-Sees validated her worth. It opened her eyes to a God who, unlike the cruel gods of Egypt, actually cared about her. It introduced her to a Deity who not only concerned Himself with her plight, but planned to use it to bless her.

Those are some world-rocking revelations for a little Egyptian girl living in Old Testament times.

But you know what? She never would have received them if she hadn't been wounded. She would have missed out on them all if she hadn't been driven by disappointment straight into the arms of the God-Who-Sees.

Much the same thing could be said about us, I suppose. Our stories are different than Hagar's; our wildernesses a little more civilized. Yet it's often when we're running from pain that we stumble into our Father's lap. It's when life's injustices bring us staggering to our knees that we're most likely to look up and find ourselves gazing more intimately into the eyes of God.

I discovered that fact in a very personal way one devastating day 25 years ago. Sitting in a hotel room with Robert, I heard the news no wife ever wants to hear: My husband had been unfaithful. As his confession unfolded, I could scarcely believe it. *I don't deserve this! I thought. How can it be happening?* I'd been a good wife—not perfect, no—but loving. And *always* faithful.

My heart throbbing with pain, I wanted to run away like Hagar did. But I had no desert in which I could disappear. So grabbing the Gideon's Bible from the nightstand, I took the only available escape. I fled to the bathroom where I cried and prayed for the rest of the night.

Alone as I've ever been, I had no one to turn to and no one to talk to but the Lord. So, asking His guidance, I opened the Bible. Genesis 50:20 was the first verse I saw. It was a familiar scripture from the story of Joseph where he explained to his brothers that their mistreatment of him had achieved a divine purpose. "But as for you, you meant evil against me;" he said, "but God meant it for good."

God meant it for good.

I knew immediately those words were for me. The Lord had spoken them to me at that moment as surely as He'd spoken to Sarah's maid in the wilderness. I sensed His presence and felt His peace wrap around me like a father's strong arm. As I wiped away my tears, I couldn't see how this awful betrayal could ever turn out for my good, but I chose to believe it anyway. And believing brought me the courage to go on.

In the weeks that followed, I found myself seeking God at a whole new level. I stepped into a grace so sweet and sustained that He seemed moment-by-moment as close as my next breath. Every day I sang to myself, "The steadfast love of the Lord never ceases," and the Lord confirmed in my heart it was true.

Robert had let me down, but the Lord hadn't. In fact, He was lifting me higher, closer to Him than I'd ever been before.

To be clear, I'm not saying God made everything easy for me. He required of me the same kind of hard obedience He required of Hagar. Just as He directed her to return to Abraham and Sarah and the place of her mistreatment, God directed me to forgive Robert and stay committed to our marriage.

To do so, I had to receive some major revelations. I had to

realize in a whole new way that Robert and I are one; we're joined together in the Lord. It's not a revelation I particularly wanted at the time, but I'll always be glad I got it. It helped me in so many ways. It especially affected the way I prayed. I began to see that if God judged Robert for his sin, the judgment would affect me too—and I didn't deserve judgment, I deserved mercy! So I prayed for us, not as individuals but as a couple.

Even though I hadn't been a part of his sin, I identified with my husband like the Old Testament intercessors identified with the sins of Israel. My prayers didn't override his need and responsibility to repent, of course. But with a fresh understanding that Robert and I are in this together, I no longer prayed for vengeance. I prayed, "God forgive us and have mercy."

Prayer, however, was only one part of the work that had to be done. For Robert and me to operate in unity, we also had to build a bridge to span the raging waters of mistrust that had come between us. That meant I needed to know some details about what had happened. (Correction: I needed to know *a lot* of details.) Without discussing it, Robert and I each made a personal commitment to communicate responsibly. He promised to honestly answer any questions I asked him while trying not to be hurtful. I promised not to ask until I was ready to hear.

To keep my commitment, I found I had to evaluate my state of mind before I asked a question. If I thought the answer would wreck me, we didn't go there. If I thought I could handle it, we did.

I hope you never need this bit of wisdom, but if you do, I trust you'll remember it: couples in these types of situations often rush to know too much too soon. They demand facts they're not yet healed enough to process and end up detonating emotional explosions that further damage their relationship. Reacting out of their pain, they hurt each other even more. That's why I say to people whose marriages are in crisis: run, don't walk, to a professional Christian counselor or pastor. Locate someone who can help you find God in the situation, someone who is committed to not only keeping you together but to getting you healed and thriving again.

Robert and I had such help, and by God's grace, we made it through. Focusing on healing and not on the wounds, we worked slowly through the pain, uncovering layer after layer, telling and hearing the truth. In time, all my questions were answered. Our mutual transparency helped heal me. Careful not to drag the process out too long, after a season, we closed the book on the betrayal, and I vowed never to bring it up again.

Difficult as that period of our life was, it marked a beautiful turning point in our marriage. Our relationship had always been close, but we'd never before been so tender and vulnerable. Intimacy is being able to tell someone the worst and know they still love you. As we opened our hearts to each other again and again, Robert and I discovered true intimacy for the first time.

Do I wish we could have found it an easier way? Yes; even now, years later, I must say that I do. But then I think about the God encounters. I remember the times in His presence singing about His steadfast love and the sweet healing touch of the God-Who-Sees-Me.

And I have to admit, I wouldn't trade those times for anything.

THE TRANSFORMATION MAKES THE PAIN WORTHWHILE

God meant it for good. He didn't cause the wounds I suffered, but He did infuse those wounds with divine purpose. Once I saw the purpose, even in the midst of the pain, I leaned into it. I realized that nothing could get to me without His permission, that I was always in His care, and I became grateful. Not for the suffering itself but for how God was transforming me through it.

In the end, such transformation is what makes our pain worthwhile. Our wounds become much more bearable when we see that each one can serve a purpose and bring forth a greater good in our life.

The Bible says, "Faithful are the wounds of a friend" (Proverbs 27:6); "Blessed is the man whom God corrects ... For he wounds, but he also binds up; he injures, but his hands also heal" (Job 5:17-18 NIV). Those are sobering scriptures, but we can see how true they are by looking at the lives of some of our greatest spiritual heroes. People like David, who was betrayed by Saul, and Joseph, who was sold into slavery by his brothers, were prepared for and directed into their divine destinies by the wounds life dealt them.

Then, of course, there was Jacob. He wrestled with God to get His blessing and ended up with a wound as well. Touched in the socket of his hip by the Lord Himself, he walked away from his wrestling match with a permanent limp and a new name. No longer a self-reliant trickster whose name meant deceiver, Jacob was transformed into the humble man named Israel, a Prince with God.

A.W. Tozier wrote, "There's nothing like a wound to take the self-assurance out of us, to reduce us to childhood again, and make us small and helpless in our own sight." That's not a common perspective these days, but in years gone by, there was at least one saint who adopted it. Her name was Lady Julian. She so treasured the way God could be found through wounds, she actually asked for them.

As Tozier tells it, she often prayed, "O God, please give me three wounds—the wound of contrition, the wound of compassion, and the wound of longing after God." Then she added this postscript. "This I ask without condition."

Although it's a wonderful prayer, I can't say I've prayed it myself. But I don't really have to, because wounds are just a part of life. We're all going to experience them whether we ask for them or not. At four years old, my grandson Grady can already confirm it: No matter how hard we may try to avoid them, hurts happen; disappointments come; the Willows in our lives sometimes wallop us for no apparent reason; and circumstances aren't always fair.

Life is a road full of bumps and potholes, unexpected twists and turns. It's a challenging and sometimes painful journey that is always moving us toward God.

DON'T MISS OUT
ON THE MIRACLES

Then Jethro took Moses' wife, Zipporah, to him (for he had sent her home).

EXODUS 18:2, TLB

"YOU THINK WE SHOULD DO WHAT?"

Y Zipporah's words hung in the air like smoke from a freshly kindled fire. Her eyes sparking with fury, she hugged baby Gershom tighter to her chest and glared at Moses.

Clearly, this was going to be a long night.

Sighing, Moses rubbed his forehead with his fingertips. He was exhausted already and the conversation had barely begun. "I promise it won't hurt him," he said. "Hebrews have been circumcising their boys for hundreds of years."

"Well, I'm not Hebrew!" Zipporah stiffened at the thought. "What's more, our son is not a slave and I don't want him identified as one."

The stubborn set of his wife's jaw stopped Moses from reminding her of his own Hebrew heritage. She preferred to think of him as a former prince of Egypt. It had always been a sore spot between them. Determined to be patient, he reminded himself how strange this whole concept must seem to a Midianite and tried again to reason with her.

"Sweetheart, you know circumcision isn't a sign of slavery. It's a sign of our covenant with God."

"You can call it whatever you want," she interrupted, her voice icy with finality, "but as far as I'm concerned, it's barbaric! And if you think I'm going to agree to it you are OUT ... OF ... YOUR ... MIND!"

Zipporah whirled on her heel and stormed out of the tent clutching their son in her arms. Moses watched her go without another word. Tongue-tied, as usual, he wondered why he always lost such arguments. Why couldn't he just take charge? Why couldn't he just tell his wife, "It's my way or the highway"?

I'm just too meek! he thought. Shrugging his shoulders, his palms upturned, he rolled his eyes heavenward. He had no idea how he would ever manage to please both God and his wife at the same time.

*   *   *

Okay, I'll admit it. I'm dramatizing a little. The Bible doesn't really say such a conversation took place between Moses and Zipporah. But reading between the lines, we almost have to assume it did. Probably more than once. The discussion might not have unfolded exactly that way, of course. I've guessed about the details. But one thing is certain, by the time Moses set out with his wife and sons to free the Israelite slaves, circumcision had long been a topic of debate.

And apparently, it was a debate Zipporah refused to let her husband win.

Considering everything she'd put up with as a wife, her resistance was reasonable. From the very beginning, married life with Moses had been a wild ride. The surprises had started early. The first day she met him—when he showed up at the well and rescued Zipporah and her sisters from the water-stealing shepherds—he said he was Egyptian. A tall dark stranger, he swept her off her feet. Then she married him, only to find out he wasn't really Egyptian at all but a kind of cultural hybrid: an Israelite slave by birth raised as royalty in Pharaoh's palace. What a confusing combination! If that wasn't weird enough, he turned out to be a fugitive running from the law because he'd killed an Egyptian for mistreating a slave.

Moses explained the murder by saying he was a divinely appointed deliverer of the Israelites. Or at least he'd once thought so. Zipporah was relieved to learn he'd abandoned the idea after burying the dead Egyptian in the sand.

No question, it was a lot for a wife to swallow. But for years, Zipporah did her best. Putting Moses' troubled past behind her, she told herself they could just live a normal Midianite life; and for a while they did. Then Moses came home from work one day with some wild-eyed tale about a perpetually burning bush.

That talked.

With the voice of God.

How was she supposed to respond to such a story? "Oh, how nice, dear. I'm glad you had an interesting day." She did try to be understanding, heaven knows. Although Moses was odd, he was also a good, humble man. That's why she was so shocked when he told her he wanted to go back to Egypt and give the whole deliver-the-Israelite-slaves thing another try. She wondered right then if he'd totally lost it. As gently as possible, she pointed out that it's not usually wise to go back to a place where you're wanted for murder—especially with the intention of causing further trouble. But Moses just kept telling her God said it would all work out and that He would go with them to make sure it did.

"The God in the bush, dear? That's the God who's going with us to Egypt?"

"Yes," he said. Then he reminded her again they should circumcise the boys before they made the trip.

Although Zipporah agreed to go back to Egypt with Moses, she put her foot down on the issue of circumcision. She didn't like it and she wasn't going to go along with it. Moses gave in to her, hoping God would understand.

As it turned out, He didn't. He was so provoked by Moses' disobedience that as the family journeyed to Egypt to deliver the Israelites (or as Zipporah thought, to face certain annihilation at the hands of Pharaoh):

> IT CAME TO PASS ON THE WAY, AT THE ENCAMPMENT,
> THAT THE LORD MET [MOSES] AND SOUGHT TO
> KILL HIM. THEN ZIPPORAH TOOK A SHARP STONE
> AND CUT OFF THE FORESKIN OF HER SON AND CAST
> IT AT MOSES' FEET, AND SAID, "SURELY YOU ARE A
> HUSBAND OF BLOOD TO ME!" (EXODUS 4:24-25)

Before I thought this story through, I was totally baffled by Zipporah's response. I couldn't figure out how she came up with circumcision as the answer. I certainly wouldn't have! If Robert and I were on our way to church and God started threatening to kill him, not in a zillion years would I guess that I could fix the problem by circumcising my sons.

But Zipporah, even though she was a gentile raised in a culture unfamiliar with the practice, didn't have to think twice about it. She knew right away what God wanted. How did she know? Her Hebrew husband had told her ... and told her ... and told her how important circumcision was. They'd had numerous conversations about it that always ended with Zipporah saying, "No!"

On the road to Egypt, however, her no changed to yes. Realizing she didn't have any other choice (except widowhood), she gave in. Her patience spent, her nerves frayed, her grace-meter on empty, she kept the letter of the law but violated the spirit of it. She did the right thing with the wrong attitude, and proved that it does not bring the desired result.

Hurling at Moses words as sharp as the stone in her hand, she threw the evidence of her obedience on the ground in front of him and said, "What a blood-smeared husband you've turned out to be!" (v. 25, TLB).

* * *

Proverbs 11:16 says, "A gracious woman retains honor." And, apparently, an ungracious woman gets sent home. That's what happened to Zipporah anyway.

After what I assume was a very ugly argument—one of those where nobody sleeps all night—Moses decided she shouldn't accompany him to Egypt. So he sent her back to Midian to her father's house where she remained until ...

WORD ... REACHED JETHRO, MOSES' FATHER-IN-LAW, THE PRIEST OF MIDIAN, ABOUT ALL THE WONDERFUL THINGS GOD HAD DONE FOR HIS PEOPLE AND FOR MOSES, AND HOW THE LORD HAD BROUGHT THEM OUT OF EGYPT. THEN JETHRO TOOK MOSES' WIFE,

Zipporah, to him (for he had sent her home), along with Moses' two sons, Gershom ... and Eliezer ... They arrived while Moses and the people were camped at Mt. Sinai.

(EXODUS 18:1—5, TLB)

Just think about everything Zipporah missed!

While she moped around home drawing water and baking bread, her husband was making history. In the prime of his ministry, he was working with God to bring the world's most powerful nation to its knees. Zipporah could have been there to see it all—the plagues plaguing, the Red Sea splitting, the Israelites marching through on dry ground, and the Egyptian army drowning behind them. She could have been witness to the most epic signs and wonders God has ever wrought on planet Earth.

But she missed it.

All because of a lousy attitude.

All because she didn't respond to a challenging situation with grace.

A NIGHT IN THE AMARILLO AIRPORT

Despite her faults, I love Zipporah. She gets me thinking about how much my bad attitudes can cost me. She reminds me of what I can miss out on if I choose to be grouchy instead of gracious when things aren't going right.

There will always be times when things don't go right. You are aware of that, aren't you? Jesus Himself warned us about it. He said, "In this world you will have trouble. But take heart! I have overcome the world" (John 16:33, NIV).

Sometimes I seem to forget that statement is in the Bible. I'll have a bad day and react with astonished resentment. Contrary circumstances will catch me off guard and, without even having an excuse as good as Zipporah's, I'll get very cranky.

I'm grateful to be able to say it happens less and less these days (to God be all the glory, I assure you), but every once in a while it still occurs. Sometimes in a big way. Like it did one terrible night at the Amarillo International Airport.

I refer to the airport by its official title because on this particular evening I arrived there so exhausted from ministry travel and so desperate to be home that even the name of the place seemed designed to annoy me. *International?* They had to be kidding. Maybe it was because the hour was late but the place was practically a ghost town. The same woman who issued us our tickets and checked our baggage showed up at the boarding gate to put us on the plane.

I was not in a frame of mind to give that woman a break, either. Regardless of how many tasks she had to attend to, I wanted her to be quick and efficient at all of them. She probably was, but my weariness warped my perceptions and she appeared to me to be moving in slow motion. Instead of attending to us at the ticket counter with a couple of clicks on her computer and whisking us on our way, she left us standing there waiting ... and waiting ... and waiting.

Internally, I begged her to hurry. *Puleeeze, just give us our tickets. All I want to do is sit down!*

When we went through airport security, the pace slowed even further. Tapping me on the shoulder, the screener motioned me aside for *special screening.* If it was indeed supposed to make me feel special, it failed. After being patted down and intruded upon in a myriad of irritating ways, I emptied out my purse and watched a stranger paw through the contents. Finally, I was waved through to the boarding gate.

I can't remember if I've ever been happier to see a chair than

I was that night. Cherishing the thought of collapsing into it and awaiting the blessed announcement that our plane was boarding, I was just about to sit down when Robert intercepted me. "Let's go over and check with the woman at the gate to see if there's anything else we need to do before departure," he said.

I looked at him like he'd suggested we race laps around the airport. Couldn't he see how tired I was? I didn't want to walk another step. "Honey, we have our tickets. Let's just sit down!"

"No, come on. Let's go check it out. Just in case."

Heartless man! Determined to do the right thing (follow my husband's instructions), I did it with a wrong attitude that became even more wrong when I realized the woman at the gate was the same one who'd served us, snail-like, at the ticket counter. Oblivious to the tick-tick-tick beside him warning that his wife-turned-time-bomb was threatening to explode, Robert smiled and asked his question. "Is there anything else we need to do?"

Long ... pause.

It wasn't a hard question, but the woman hesitated anyway. Then, reaching down to retrieve something from behind her desk, she finally answered.

"Yes."

Yes? Did she say yes? I couldn't believe it! What else could she possibly want us to do? Fill out another form? Volunteer to pass out pretzels on the flight? I couldn't take one more thing! My Zipporah moment had arrived. Gathering some sharp words, I was about to let them fly when I looked down to see what the woman held in her hand.

It was a copy of Robert's book, *The Blessed Life.*

"Will you sign this for me?" she asked him.

You've probably seen those nature shows on television where a frog snags a gnat with a flick of his tongue and gulps it down faster than the human eye can see. That's what I did with my unspoken words. In the blink of an eye, I swallowed them. Then I silently thanked God nobody ever heard them.

I still cringe to think what it might have cost if someone had.

A PHARISAICAL PITFALL

How do we avoid those kinds of Amarillo-Airport moments? How can we make sure we respond with grace when things go wrong?

The apostle Paul gives us the key in Ephesians 4.

> So I tell you this, and insist on it in the Lord, that you must no longer live as the Gentiles do, in the futility of their thinking. They are darkened in their understanding and separated from the life of God because of the ignorance that is in them due to the hardening of their hearts ... You, however, did not come to know Christ that way. Surely you heard of him and were taught in him in accordance with the truth that is in Jesus. You were taught, with regard to your former way of life, to put off your old self, which is being corrupted by its deceitful desires; to be made new in the attitude of your minds.
> (EPHESIANS 4:17-18, 21-23, NIV)

Look again at that last phrase: *Be made new in the attitude of your mind.*

That's something we absolutely must do if we want to respond graciously when we're under pressure. We must renew our attitude with a revelation of grace. We must not only know what grace is, we must have experience with it; an understanding of what it's done and continues to do for us every single day.

In other words, to extend grace to others, we must first become aware of how much grace we've received.

"But don't most of us already know that?" you might ask.

Yes, to some degree we do. We know it's by grace we're saved. We know it's by grace we're forgiven of all our sins (the big ones and the small ones). By grace, God accepted us when we didn't measure up, poured out His unmerited favor upon us, and provided a better future for us. By grace, the Almighty King, creator of heaven and earth, laid down His royal robe, came to earth, lived a perfect life and suffered a painful death just so He could have a relationship with us.

As Christians, we are fully aware that all our spiritual debts have been paid by grace.

The problem is, most of us have no idea how much we owed.

We're like the Pharisee who invited Jesus over for dinner. He was so clueless about his own spiritually impoverished condition he extended no grace to the prostitute who barged into his house to minister to the Master. As she washed Jesus' feet with her tears, dried them with her hair and anointed them with her precious, perfumed oil, the Pharisee reacted with Zipporah-like irritation. "This ... woman ... is ... a sinner!" he fumed, implying, of course, that compared to her he didn't qualify as a sinner at all, and even if he did his sin was clearly much less sinful.

Startling as it might sound, we sometimes think the same way. I certainly did. For years, I assumed that because I had gotten saved before I had time to do anything breathtakingly terrible, it didn't take as much grace to save me as it took to save a world-class sinner like Robert. Because my sin seemed relatively minimal, I figured God had expended a minimal amount of forgiveness on me.

I was mostly happy about that. I did fret about it sometimes, though, especially when I'd look at Robert and see his love for the Lord. His passion always seemed much greater than mine. Trying to figure out why, I'd think of the Pharisee and how ...

JESUS ANSWERED AND SAID TO HIM, "SIMON, I HAVE SOMETHING TO SAY TO YOU." SO HE SAID, "TEACHER, SAY IT." "THERE WAS A CERTAIN CREDITOR WHO HAD TWO DEBTORS. ONE OWED FIVE HUNDRED DENARII, AND THE OTHER FIFTY. AND WHEN THEY HAD NOTHING WITH WHICH TO REPAY, HE FREELY FORGAVE THEM BOTH. TELL ME, THEREFORE, WHICH OF THEM WILL LOVE HIM MORE?" SIMON ANSWERED AND SAID, "I SUPPOSE THE ONE WHOM HE FORGAVE MORE." AND HE SAID TO HIM, "YOU HAVE RIGHTLY JUDGED." THEN HE TURNED TO THE WOMAN AND SAID TO SIMON, "DO YOU SEE THIS WOMAN? I ENTERED YOUR HOUSE; YOU GAVE ME NO WATER FOR MY FEET, BUT SHE HAS WASHED MY FEET WITH HER TEARS AND WIPED THEM WITH THE HAIR OF HER HEAD. YOU GAVE ME NO KISS, BUT THIS WOMAN HAS NOT CEASED TO KISS MY FEET SINCE THE TIME I CAME IN. YOU DID NOT ANOINT MY HEAD WITH OIL, BUT THIS WOMAN HAS ANOINTED MY FEET WITH FRAGRANT OIL. THEREFORE I SAY TO YOU, HER SINS, WHICH ARE MANY, ARE FORGIVEN, FOR SHE LOVED MUCH. BUT TO WHOM LITTLE IS FORGIVEN, THE SAME LOVES LITTLE." (LUKE 7:40-47)

For decades, I thought Jesus was saying what I already knew to be true: Some people (like Robert) have big sin debts. Some people (like me) have little ones. And the big debtors will always love God more than the little debtors.

Although the concept made sense, it frustrated me. So I began to pray, "Lord, I want to love You as much as Robert does!"

The way God answered my prayer forever changed my perspective. He gave me a vision of myself wearing a pristine white wedding dress and running to meet Jesus. My heart was rejoicing, knowing I was the bride of Christ, but in my hurry to reach Him I fell into a mud puddle. In an instant, my dress was ruined. My hair, my skin, every part of me was drenched with mud. Crouching on my hands and knees, I wept over my filthy condition.

As I cried, the Lord revealed to me the reality of the filth in my own life. He showed me the inner rebellion and ungodly attitudes I had, even as a child. He showed me just how sinful I really was before I got saved. "I'm so dirty!" I sobbed.

Then, in the midst of my tears, I saw someone had stepped into the mud puddle with me. I looked at His feet, saw the nail prints, and realized it was Jesus. Standing in the mud yet still clean, He reached out His hand to me. As I took it, the mud that had covered me began to fall away. I stood up again, as clean as the Master Himself. Glancing back down at the mud puddle, I saw it had turned to gold ... and together, Jesus and I danced on streets of gold.

For the first time in my life, I understood the overwhelming grace God had extended toward me.

But I'm not the only one who got the revelation. Sometime later, Robert got it too. One afternoon he came running out of his study waving his Bible and proclaiming the good news. "Debbie, you weren't any better than I was before you got saved! I've found proof of it in the Bible! You needed God's grace just as much as I did!"

Explaining he'd been reading the parable of the two debtors, he told me how he'd realized both of them were in the same condition: They both owed. They both had nothing with which to pay. And they both were freely forgiven.

"The point of the parable isn't that some people are better than others!" he said. "The point is that although some people think they're better than others, we are all equally bankrupt before God!"

It's a truth the Bible confirms again and again:

- There is none righteous, no, not one; there is none who understands; there is none who seeks after God. They have all turned aside; they have together become unprofitable; there is none who does good, no, not one (Romans 3:10-12).
- For there is no difference; for all have sinned and fall short of the glory of God (vv. 22-23).
- For whoever keeps the whole law and yet stumbles at just one point is guilty of breaking all of it (James 2:10, NIV).

Some people might consider those verses sad, but to me they're thrilling. They tell me I've been forgiven of just as much as everybody else. Which means I can love Jesus as much as anybody on earth—including Robert!

CELEBRATING EVERY STEP OF THE WAY

Actually, now that I know how much grace I've received, I not only love the Lord with greater passion, I love people more too. Having experienced how gracious God has been to me, I have a heart to extend His grace to others.

There was a time when I'd see a young lady walking down the street dressed in a way I felt was inappropriate and I'd be judgmental of her. Without knowing anything about her situation, I assumed negative things about her character. It never occurred to me she might have just gotten saved. She might be a baby believer, too busy learning the basics of God's love to worry about her wardrobe.

Now I can see how legalistic and graceless my attitude actually was. I've come to understand God isn't looking at externals. He isn't focused on what people are wearing. He's looking at their hearts. He's reaching out to them with love and acceptance no matter how imperfect they might be.

Just as Zipporah's ungracious attitude caused her to miss out on seeing the miracles of God, mine would have cost me the same thing if I'd hung onto it. My legalistic, judgmental perspective would have alienated people who were in the early stages of their pilgrimage with the Lord. Expecting them to advance spiritually from A to Z overnight, I would have missed the wonder of cheering them on through the messy yet amazing growth process that takes place between B and Y. My disapproving attitude would have driven them away. I wouldn't have witnessed the miracles that happened as they took their first tiny steps toward God.

I'm sure this is true of everyone, but it's especially true of women. Apart from God's grace, we tend to view ourselves either too highly, thinking we're better than others and standing above them, or too lowly, thinking others are better than we are and using jealousy, gossip, or backbiting to pull them down.

But when we see ourselves as extensions of God's grace, we're neither above nor below anyone else. We're just who we are. Loving other women regardless of how delightful or difficult they may be, we find beauty in them. We can celebrate their strengths and abilities without criticizing and without competing. I see it happening at Gateway more and more: Women supporting, honoring and praising each other. Women rejoicing when it's someone else's turn to speak, or lead praise and worship, or go on a mission trip. Women pulling each other into the spotlight and saying, "It's your moment to shine!"

As equal recipients of God's great grace, we're realizing we don't have to feel threatened when we see a woman who's gifted in different areas than we are. Her strengths don't diminish us, and our strengths don't diminish her. On the contrary, we can benefit from each other, rejoice in our uniqueness, and reflect back to each other the grace we've all received from God.

Is it really possible for women—as notoriously evil as we can be to each other—to maintain such an attitude?

Yes! It's not only possible, it's what the Bible tells us to do. Philippians 2:5-8 (TLB) says:

> Your attitude should be the kind that was shown us by Jesus Christ, who, though he was God, did not demand and cling to his rights as God, but laid aside his mighty power and glory, taking the disguise of a slave and becoming like men. And he humbled himself even further, going so far as actually to die a criminal's death on a cross.

JUST GRAB A SPOON

Granted, sustaining a Christ-like attitude toward one another can be a challenge at times. As I've already mentioned and Zipporah has demonstrated, things don't always go right. Sometimes we get tired and circumstances aggravate us. Sometimes people upset us, act unkindly toward us, and even persecute us. At those moments, we all wish we had an "Easy Button" to push that would make it more comfortable for us to dispense God's grace.

But there is no Easy Button. Just as going to the cross wasn't easy for Jesus, extending grace when we're exhausted or hurt or frustrated won't always be easy for us. But by the power of God, we can do it if we'll predetermine that's the choice we're going to make.

A few years ago, before my daughter Elaine went off to college, Robert and I talked to her a lot about predetermined choices. We encouraged her to think through the situations she might encounter at school and asked, "Are you going to drink? How late will you stay out at night? What times will you set aside for studying?" We knew she'd be better off if she pre-made those decisions.

That's not just true for college girls; it's true for every life-giving woman. We should pre-make our decision to be extenders of God's grace. We should predetermine that if our husband doesn't pick up after himself (and we know he won't) we'll be gracious about it. Thinking through the various possibilities—if someone is rude to us at church, our co-worker at the office criticizes our report, or our already svelte neighbor tells us on a day we feel especially bloated she just lost 10 pounds—we should decide beforehand we will respond with grace.

Oh, what a difference such decisions can make! They can turn messes into memories and fiascos into fun. I saw it for myself the day my mom lost her grip on the pie plate when I was a little girl. I'll never forget it. She'd spent the whole day cleaning house from top to bottom because guests were coming. Everything was ready except for the pie. One of those cream cheese affairs in a graham cracker crust with cherry topping; it was assembled but still needed to chill for a while. As my sister and I watched, mouths watering, my mom lifted the pie from the counter to put it in the refrigerator when tragedy struck. The pie took a tumble and went splat on her sparkling clean kitchen floor.

For one awful moment, all three of us stared at it in shock. Then, with great grace, my mom reached into the silverware drawer and took out three spoons. "Let's eat!" she said with a grin. So we all sat down and had a pie party on the floor. Leaving enough cream cheese on the linoleum to protect us from germs, we ate all we wanted, cleaned up the rest and had a great day.

It's a memory I'll always cherish. And it happened because my mother chose to be gracious, not grouchy. She decided that instead of making a big deal out of the mess, she'd do what Jesus would do (if He ever dropped a pie) and covered the whole situation with forgiveness and love.

Really, when you get right down to it, that's what grace is. It's doing for others what Jesus has already done for us. It's obeying the instructions in 1 Peter 4:1-2:

> THEREFORE, SINCE CHRIST SUFFERED FOR US IN THE FLESH, ARM YOURSELVES ALSO WITH THE SAME MIND, FOR HE WHO HAS SUFFERED IN THE FLESH HAS CEASED FROM SIN, THAT HE NO LONGER SHOULD LIVE THE REST OF HIS TIME IN THE FLESH FOR THE LUSTS OF MEN, BUT FOR THE WILL OF GOD.

When we arm ourselves in advance with the decision that we're going to follow Christ's example and suffer if necessary rather than act ungraciously, we put God's will above our own. We open the door for Him to move in wonderful ways not only in our own lives, but in the lives of others as well.

Sometimes the grace we extend will leave a small but lasting impression on someone. It will do for them what my mother's pie party did for me. Other times, our graciousness will make the kind of major difference that changes a life completely.

A few years ago, a well-known Bible teacher described such a time when she ministered at Gateway. She told us about a grace-challenge she faced when she preached on the subject of divine healing at a particular church. The service went well, or so she thought, but when she finished her message the pastor of the church stepped to the pulpit and refuted everything she'd said.

She was stunned. She'd asked him in advance about the teaching she planned to deliver and he'd given her his blessing. Sitting frozen on the front row, listening to him tell the congregation how wrong she was, she felt humiliated, betrayed, and angry.

But in the midst of it all, the Holy Spirit spoke to her heart. "The message everyone will remember is the look on your face right now," He said.

It was true. She knew it. So instead of walking out in a huff as she so desperately wanted to do, she plastered a great big smile on her face.

Do you know what happened next?

To everyone's astonishment, the healing power of God broke out right there in the service. Remarkable healings took place. Miracles happened. Miracles everyone would have missed if she had responded with an attitude like Zipporah's instead of an attitude of grace.

CHAPTER 7

THE BIG "S"

The king's heart is in the hand of the LORD, like the rivers of water; He turns it wherever He wishes.

PROVERBS 21:1

SHE FIRST SCURRIED ACROSS American television screens in the 1970s. Ever dowdy in house dress and apron, her mouse-colored hair in a frizzled state of alarm, she quickly became the symbol of everything contemporary women do *not* want to be.

Answering the bellows of her barcalounging husband with her signature screech *"Coming, Archie!"*, she surrendered spinelessly to his constant demands. She made muddle-headed excuses for his inexcusable behavior. Sweet but scatterbrained, she wielded no power in the world and exerted precious little influence even in her own home. And even as she made us laugh, she left us with an image of submission scary enough to send any sane woman screaming in terror in the opposite direction.

Nobody in their right mind wants to be Edith Bunker.

Which is why, the last time I spoke on submission, I initially told the group we were going to talk about the "Big S." When everybody smiled and seemed eager to hear more, I knew they were thinking about a different S-word. The topic of submission rarely generates such an enthusiastic response. Along with hair curlers, girdles, and non-microwaveable cookware, it's gone out of style and many women hope it will never be back.

I can understand why. The old school image of submission just doesn't fit our 21st century mindset. Women these days, whether homemakers or corporate executives, want to be world-changers and culture shapers. We aim to advance the kingdom of God, build strong families, bless multitudes, impact the political scene, create jobs, and champion causes that enrich people's lives.

How on earth can we succeed at such things and still be submissive at the same time?

Believe it or not, I can answer that question with a single word. Esther.

One of the most amazing women in the Bible, Esther provided permanent proof of just how powerful an attitude of submission can be. Her influence mightily affected not only a king but a kingdom so massive it stretched from India to Ethiopia. Her wisdom changed the laws of a nation. Her intervention prevented genocide and saved the Jewish race. In other words, Esther, although famous for her graceful submission to the authorities in her life, was no Edith Bunker.

But then, she was no Queen Vashti, either.

Esther's predecessor in the palace of King Ahasuerus, Queen Vashti lost her crown when she took a stand common in our day but rare in hers: she refused to submit to her husband. When he asked her to join him at a royal banquet, she declined and indicated she had better things to do.

The Bible doesn't tell us why she did it. I'm sure she thought her reasons were good. Maybe she didn't want to leave the party she was hosting for the women in the royal palace. Maybe she didn't feel like putting up with her husband's friends. Maybe she was tired or had a headache. Whatever her excuse, it didn't sit well with the king, and he consulted his advisors about what to do. After discussing her disrespectful behavior, they came to this consensus.

> "QUEEN VASHTI HAS NOT ONLY WRONGED THE KING, BUT ALSO ALL THE PRINCES, AND ALL THE PEOPLE WHO ARE IN ALL THE PROVINCES OF KING AHASUERUS. FOR THE QUEEN'S BEHAVIOR WILL BECOME KNOWN TO ALL WOMEN, SO THAT THEY WILL DESPISE THEIR HUSBANDS IN THEIR EYES ... LET IT BE RECORDED IN THE LAWS OF THE PERSIANS AND THE MEDES, SO THAT IT WILL NOT BE ALTERED, THAT VASHTI SHALL COME NO MORE BEFORE KING AHASUERUS; AND LET THE KING GIVE HER ROYAL POSITION TO ANOTHER WHO IS BETTER THAN SHE. WHEN THE KING'S DECREE WHICH HE WILL MAKE IS PROCLAIMED THROUGHOUT ALL HIS EMPIRE (FOR IT IS GREAT), ALL WIVES WILL HONOR THEIR HUSBANDS, BOTH GREAT AND SMALL." (ESTHER 1:16-20)

Apparently, Persia wasn't ready for a nation full of defiant domestic divas. So Vashti exited the scene without her crown, and the search for her replacement began.

When Esther was chosen as a possibility, everybody in the palace must have found her refreshing. A sharp contrast to Vashti, she'd been taught by her uncle Mordecai, who raised her after her parents died, to be respectful and submissive. Her attitude quickly paved the way for her advancement and she became a favorite with the royal staff. Everybody loved her. Especially the king, who "set the royal crown upon her head and made her queen instead of Vashti" (Esther 2:17).

AND THEY ALMOST LIVED HAPPILY EVER AFTER

It sounds like a fairy tale ending, except for one thing: it's just the first chapter of the story. What happened next marks one of the most chilling episodes in Jewish history. You can find the full account of it in the Book of Esther, but the short version boils down to this: Not long after their wedding, Esther's new husband was tricked by a wicked government official named Haman into signing an edict calling for the extermination of every Jewish man, woman, and child in the Medo-Persian empire.

No one in the palace knew that Esther was a Jew. In obedience to Mordecai's instructions, she hadn't told them. She had reason to believe she might be safe from the slaughter if she'd only lay low and keep quiet. Mordecai, however, sent word telling her to do just the opposite. "Go in to the king to make supplication to him and plead before him for your people," he instructed.

Easier said than done. The king hadn't called for Esther in 30 days. According to law, anyone—the queen included—who went into the throne room uninvited would be executed unless the king made an exception by extending to them his golden scepter.

Esther explained the danger to Mordecai, but he expressed no sympathy. "Do not think in your heart that you will escape in the king's palace any more than all the other Jews," he said. "For if you remain completely silent at this time, relief and deliverance will arise for the Jews from another place, but you and your father's house will perish. Yet who knows whether you have come to the kingdom for such a time as this?" (Esther 4:13-14).

Shattering the old school stereotype, Esther's response to Mordecai, although submissive, was neither scatterbrained nor spineless.

> "Go, gather all the Jews who are present in Shushan, and fast for me; neither eat nor drink for three days, night or day. My maids and I will fast likewise. And so I will go to the king, which is against the law; and if I perish, I perish!" (V. 16)

NOT JUST FOR WOMEN AND DEFINITELY NOT FOR WIMPS

Forget Edith Bunker. Women who submit the way Esther did aren't wimps. They're women of faith. They're courageous believers who know the Bible says, "The king's heart is in the hand of the LORD, like the rivers of water; He turns it wherever He wishes" (Proverbs 21:1). They're gutsy gals who trust God to move in the hearts of the authorities in their lives and work things out for their good.

I know what you're probably thinking. You've seen women who've been bullied into submission. Cringing and kowtowing to their husband or their boss, they obey out of fear not faith. But there's a big difference between obeying and submitting. Obedience can be forced. Submission can't. It's an attitude, not just an action, and to be genuine it must spring from a willing heart.

When I drive within the speed limit because there's a policeman nearby who might give me a ticket, that's obedience. When I observe the speed limit because I honor the law, whether or not there's a policeman around, that's submission. And it's not just for women. Everybody who wants to get their prayers answered and receive from God must know how to submit.

Even Roman centurions.

Read Matthew 8 and you'll see what I mean. It tells about a Roman centurion who approached Jesus and asked Him to heal his servant. When Jesus answered, "I will come and heal him," the centurion replied:

> "LORD, I AM NOT WORTHY THAT YOU SHOULD COME UNDER MY ROOF. BUT ONLY SPEAK A WORD, AND MY SERVANT WILL BE HEALED. FOR I ALSO AM A MAN UNDER AUTHORITY, HAVING SOLDIERS UNDER ME. AND I SAY TO THIS ONE, 'GO,' AND HE GOES; AND TO ANOTHER, 'COME,' AND HE COMES; AND TO MY SERVANT, 'DO THIS,' AND HE DOES IT." WHEN JESUS HEARD IT, HE MARVELED, AND SAID TO THOSE WHO FOLLOWED, "ASSUREDLY, I SAY TO YOU, I HAVE NOT FOUND SUCH GREAT FAITH, NOT EVEN IN ISRAEL!"
> **(MATTHEW 8:8-10)**

Notice Jesus' response: "I will come and heal him." He didn't say, "I don't care about servants." He didn't say, "I want him to die because people will get saved at his funeral." No, it's God's will to heal and save. He wants to work miracles. But for us to experience those miracles, we need to understand authority like the centurion did.

He knew that everybody on earth, including Jesus, is part of a chain of command. He'd learned in the Roman army that submitting to authority gives a soldier authority himself. *I have someone over me, therefore, I have someone under me,* he reasoned. *I'm under authority, therefore I have authority.*

According to Jesus, that revelation was a key to the centurion's great faith. It made him confident in Jesus' right to release divine power on his behalf. He reasoned that since Jesus was submitted to God and he was submitted to Jesus, heaven's blessings could freely flow. As a result, his servant was healed that same hour (Matthew 8:13).

Whether you're a soldier, a servant, or a beauty queen, submission is a good thing.

It not only brings us divine promotion like it did for Esther and positions us to receive God's power, like it did for the centurion, it also protects us.

I can't count the number of times submitting to Robert Morris has saved me from hurt, trouble, or embarrassment. Or the times I didn't submit and regretted it—like the day a few years ago when we were driving home from a meeting in west Texas. Robert, worn out from preaching, had asked me to drive. As I slid behind the steering wheel he said to me, "Don't speed."

I agreed, of course, in theory.

Then I set the cruise control at 67. Granted, this was slightly faster than the posted speed limit of 65. But I was certain I could get away with it. So certain, in fact, I didn't even tap the brake when I passed a highway patrol car on the side of the road—until I saw the lights flashing in my mirror.

Mercifully, the officer only issued me a warning instead of a ticket. But even so, once he stepped out of earshot, I expressed my indignation. "That's ridiculous!" I said. "I was only going 67!"

Robert just looked at me. "I told you not to speed," he said.

It was a trivial incident, but it illustrates a significant spiritual fact: When we step out from under our delegated authority, our faith is weakened, our own authority is undermined, and we become open prey for the enemy. (Not that I'm suggesting the highway patrol is the enemy.) Therefore, if we want to live in victory, we must learn to submit to the authority structure of God.

Jesus Himself showed us how. His entire life on earth was one of subjection and submission not only to His heavenly Father, but to earthly authorities as well.

- As a young boy living with his parents, he "was subject to them" (Luke 2:51).
- He submitted to water baptism by John even though He had no need of it (Matthew 3:15).
- He submitted to the religious rulers and paid the Temple tax, although as the Son of God He should have been exempt from it (Matthew 17:27).
- He submitted to the Roman government and taught his fellow Jews to "Render to Caesar the things that are Caesar's" (Mark 12:17).
- He told His disciples to submit to the Scribes and Pharisees because they occupied Moses' seat of authority (Matthew 23:3).
- He subjected Himself to God and to the cross by praying the ultimate prayer of submission: "Father, if it is Your will, take this cup away from Me; nevertheless not My will, but Yours, be done" (Luke 22:42).

A DANCE NOT A MARCH

Although it's gotten a bad rap, submission carried out according to God's design is actually beautiful, especially between a husband and wife. It provides order in the home. (God gives order to everything

He cares about. He ordained an order for creation, an order for the Church, and an order for marriage.) But it's not a rigid order or an authoritarian military-like march.

Godly submission in marriage is more like a dance, a waltz. If each person excels in their role, it's impossible to detect who's directing the steps. The husband leads and the wife follows, but they appear to move as one. "Submitting to one another in the fear of God," they flex and flow with each other as they follow the Scriptural instructions:

> WIVES, SUBMIT TO YOUR OWN HUSBANDS, AS TO THE
> LORD. FOR THE HUSBAND IS HEAD OF THE WIFE, AS
> ALSO CHRIST IS HEAD OF THE CHURCH; AND HE IS
> THE SAVIOR OF THE BODY. THEREFORE, JUST AS THE
> CHURCH IS SUBJECT TO CHRIST, SO LET THE WIVES
> BE TO THEIR OWN HUSBANDS IN EVERYTHING. ... SO
> HUSBANDS OUGHT TO LOVE THEIR OWN WIVES AS
> THEIR OWN BODIES; HE WHO LOVES HIS WIFE LOVES
> HIMSELF. FOR NO ONE EVER HATED HIS OWN FLESH,
> BUT NOURISHES AND CHERISHES IT, JUST AS THE
> LORD DOES THE CHURCH. (EPHESIANS 5:22-29)

God gave us those instructions not to hurt us but to help us. Perhaps if sin had never entered the picture and Adam hadn't fallen, we wouldn't need an authority structure in marriage. Our wills would be so completely united with God's and with each other that submission would be a moot point. But because of the fall we each ended up with an individual will and we need a plan to keep things running smoothly when we disagree. So God gave us one. It's not an evil plan; it's a good one. It's for our benefit.

Under God's plan, when a husband and wife can't agree about something and a decision must be made, then the husband bears the responsibility—he has to make the decision. That doesn't mean, however, the wife should withhold her opinion, put on a happy face, and just march onward like a little Christian soldier trying to make it through.

I used to think that's what submission required, and I made some mistakes as a result. The most costly one I made was the year Robert and I moved our son, James, to a new Christian school. We'd heard great things about the school and it checked out fine, but I never felt peace about it. I kept sensing in my heart that public education might be a better choice.

The Christian school was expensive and we had to pay up front for the entire year. On the day of enrollment, Robert and I drove to the school and wrote the check. It represented a lot of money to us at the time—it still does, come to think of it—and I thought we might be making a mistake. But I didn't communicate my misgivings to Robert.

You can guess what happened. It turned out to be a disaster. The first semester was terrible and at Christmas we transferred our son to a public school (where he did quite well, by the way). A tough lesson to learn, it taught me that Robert needs my viewpoint. He needs me to be a part of the decision making process. Although he has the final say in our family, he's not meant to be a lone ranger. God has given me to him as a helpmate. If I don't share my opinions, concerns, and insights, he lacks part of the understanding God wants him to have.

* * *

Although it's sad to say, some husbands don't value their wives as helpmates. Some even try to use the scriptural concept of submission to dominate and control. So I want to make this very clear: the Bible does not condone authoritarianism and it does not require a woman to submit to abuse of any kind—physical or psychological. Wives should always have the freedom to lovingly yield to their husbands' leadership by choice, not because they've been pressured or forced. In a marriage, that's the only atmosphere in which genuine submission can thrive.

What's more, God's Word is always a woman's final authority. If her husband asks her to do something she believes is sinful, she not only has the right but the responsibility to say no. That's what Sapphira should have done in Acts 5. When Ananias came up with the idea of lying about the offering they gave to the church, she should have refused to go along with him. But she didn't, and it cost her her life.

When issues of sin are involved, Christian women need to set a standard in their homes. They should say, "No, that's not acceptable. If you choose to do it, I don't want to be a part of it." If a husband wants to bring pornography into the relationship, for example, the wife should draw the line. She doesn't have to be self-righteous about it. She can just explain that it's wrong and detrimental to true intimacy.

Then she can suggest some other ways to heat up the bedroom that will not only foster and support real relationship but will also be a lot more fun. She can say, "Believe me, honey, we don't need sinful stuff to have fun. We can have a rocking good time without it!" Of course, to make good on such a promise, both wife and husband must put forth some effort. Genuine romance takes energy. If you're going to have a wild night without the ungodly props the world provides, you'll have to participate at a higher level. But, that's okay.

The payoff is definitely worth the price.

A CRASH COURSE IN APPEALS

If you want to excel at the divine art of submission, the first thing you'll need is a crash course in making appeals. According to the dictionary, an appeal is an earnest request, an entreaty, or petition directed to a person in authority regarding a decision or judgment. It's an avenue we can use to present our requests, share our insights and voice our opinions in the most effective way while still maintaining a gracious, submissive attitude.

When it comes to making appeals, Esther is definitely the queen.

But of course, she had to be. When she presented her appeal to King Ahasureus on behalf of the Jewish people it was a matter of life or death. She couldn't afford to mess it up. She had to make sure she used her influence with the king wisely. That's why she didn't just rush into the interaction without thinking. Instead, she prepared for it. She sought God's wisdom, assistance, and anointing through prayer and fasting.

In doing so, she set a wonderful example for the rest of us to follow. Granted, we'll rarely need to pray and fast for three days like she did before approaching our boss or our husband about an issue (even an important one), but we should always ask the Lord to help us and show us the best way to handle our appeals.

In my own life, I've found I don't have to be scared to submit to whatever my authority decides as long as I know God is involved. After all, He loves me. He's concerned about the details of my life, and He's watching out for me. He also holds the heart of the king (a.k.a. my husband and every other authority) in His hand, and He can turn it any way He wants. So if I pray, I can be confident He'll work things out to my advantage.

I'm sure Esther felt the same way. Her prayers brought her confidence in the midst of a potentially frightening situation. They helped her hear from God about exactly what she should do and say. Maybe during those days of seeking God and fasting, she stood in front of the mirror and rehearsed for her meeting with the king. Maybe she came up with several ways to approach him and sought the Lord's counsel about which was the best. Whatever she did, we know this for sure: she received the guidance she needed and "... it happened on the third day that Esther put on her royal robes and stood in the inner court of the king's palace, across from the king's house, while the king sat on his royal throne ..." (Esther 5:1).

Notice, Esther presented herself to the king in a pleasing way. She came before him with beauty and dignity as a person of influence. She didn't shuffle into the throne room in her bathrobe and slippers with ashes of mourning on her head. She came in with a positive attitude and a pleasing countenance.

You and I will have more success with our appeals if we do the same. Our attitude and countenance make a big difference in how we're received. If we go into a conversation with our husbands or a meeting with our bosses wearing a scowl and acting pouty, we're likely to run into resistance. If we go in all smiles and sweetness, we're likely to be greeted with favor.

When I have a good attitude it seems I can say and do almost anything and still come out okay. But when my attitude is wrong, no matter how right my words and actions might be, I get in trouble.

Bad attitudes always come back to bite us.

So does bad timing. That's why Esther didn't go storming into the king's royal court the instant she found out about the edict he'd signed. She waited until the third day.

When it comes to influencing people, it's not just *what* we say that counts, it's *when* we say it. Timing is important. Choosing the right moment to talk to someone gives us a much better chance of being heard. It gains us more favor. When Elaine was a teenager, I used to tell her, "Timing is everything!" But she rarely heeded my advice. She invariably made her appeals to Robert just as he walked in the door after a long, tiring day. Before he could even say hello, she'd hit him with a request for money or ask him for the car keys or lobby for permission to go somewhere on Friday night. Often his response was not what she'd hoped.

"Elaine, just give him a few minutes to catch his breath," I'd tell her. "Wait for him to rest and relax a little. Then sweetly go ask him for what you want and you'll get so much more!" She didn't usually listen to me, though. She's too much like him. She wants to get things done *now*.

But, as we must all eventually learn, *now* isn't always the right time.

When Robert and I are driving to church and he's about to preach, for instance, I've found it's best not to bring up certain subjects. That's not the right moment to ask for money, or share my dreams, or chat about random concerns. Even though I have a few minutes alone with him and he's quiet, his silence means he's thinking about the service; it does not mean he's wondering what's on my mind.

If I wait until he's preached and had some time to wind down, I can talk to him about anything and he'll be much more responsive. He'll pay attention and listen to me and, as you can imagine, that's much more gratifying for both of us.

QUESTIONS AND ANSWERS

Apparently, Esther's timing was perfect because when the king saw her standing in the court:

SHE FOUND FAVOR IN HIS SIGHT, AND THE KING HELD OUT TO ESTHER THE GOLDEN SCEPTER THAT WAS IN HIS HAND. THEN ESTHER WENT NEAR AND TOUCHED THE TOP OF THE SCEPTER. AND THE KING SAID TO HER, "WHAT DO YOU WISH, QUEEN ESTHER? WHAT IS YOUR REQUEST? IT SHALL BE GIVEN TO YOU; UP TO HALF THE KINGDOM!" SO ESTHER ANSWERED, "IF IT PLEASES THE KING, LET THE KING AND HAMAN COME TODAY TO THE BANQUET THAT I HAVE PREPARED FOR HIM." (ESTHER 5:2-4)

Surprising, isn't it? Here Esther gets an opportunity to express her grievances in a direct way to the king, but she refrains and chooses an indirect approach: she issues an invitation. She asks the king to a dinner party and suggests he bring the murderous Haman along.

The king accepted her invitation. He brought Haman to dinner and asked Esther a second time, "What is your petition? It shall be granted you," he said. "What is your request, up to half the kingdom? It shall be done!" (v. 6).

Once again, rather than blurting out her appeal, Esther asked the king and Haman to come to yet another banquet the following night. Then she added, "And tomorrow I will do as the king has said" (v. 8).

Here's what Esther understood that we all need to learn: confronting issues head on isn't always the best plan. It's often easier to influence a person in authority and maintain a humble, submissive attitude by asking questions.

I've certainly found it to be true in my own life. When Robert and I don't see eye to eye about something, instead of hammering him with my opposing viewpoint, I prefer to ask him quality questions. Sometimes they help him consider the issue from my perspective.

Other times they help me to better understand (and thus cooperate with) his perspective. Either way, I've found questions to be highly beneficial, so I encourage you to use them.

Say, for instance, your husband announces with great excitement he's going to buy a new computer, and you can't see how it fits into the budget. Before you tell him it's a bad idea, ask him some questions. Find out what sparked his desire for the computer. Ask him how he plans to use it. Ask him if there's a way to trim the family budget so the expense won't end up being a financial challenge.

Be sure your questions are supportive, though. Don't use them to attack or criticize. Say something like, "Honey, I can see this is important to you and I want you to have it. I'd just like us to think through any potential problems in advance."

Once you've asked your questions, give him time to consider them. Let him frame his thoughts without any pressure from you. When I do that with Robert, sometimes he'll totally forget what I asked him. Then a day or two later, a light bulb will come on and he'll see my point and think it was his own idea. That's okay with me. I just stay quiet and rejoice that he has the answer he needs (and it's an answer with which I happen to agree).

I'm not suggesting, of course, we should use questions as a means of manipulation. Our goal in asking should never be to get our own way or control the outcome of the situation. What we want is merely to help the other person connect more thoroughly with their heart and mind. As long as we are trusting God to speak to them and direct them according to His will, manipulation will be the farthest thing from our mind.

JUST THE FACTS, MA'AM

SO THE KING AND HAMAN WENT TO DINE WITH
QUEEN ESTHER. AND ON THE SECOND DAY, AT THE
BANQUET OF WINE, THE KING AGAIN SAID TO ES-
THER, "WHAT IS YOUR PETITION, QUEEN ESTHER?
IT SHALL BE GRANTED YOU. AND WHAT IS YOUR
REQUEST, UP TO HALF THE KINGDOM? IT SHALL BE
DONE!" THEN QUEEN ESTHER ANSWERED AND SAID,
"IF I HAVE FOUND FAVOR IN YOUR SIGHT, O KING,
AND IF IT PLEASES THE KING, LET MY LIFE BE GIVEN
ME AT MY PETITION, AND MY PEOPLE AT MY RE-
QUEST. FOR WE HAVE BEEN SOLD, MY PEOPLE AND I,
TO BE DESTROYED, TO BE KILLED, AND TO BE ANNIHI-
LATED." (ESTHER 7:1-4A)

Do you know what stands out to me in these verses about the way Esther finally presented her appeal? She didn't beat around the bush. She got straight to the point. I think I know why: King Ahaseurus was a bottom-line guy. Like Sgt. Friday (and most other men), he preferred to hear, "Just the facts, ma'am." So that's what Esther gave him.

I can relate. My husband is a Sgt. Friday, too. I can't load him up with all the details and expect him to dig through them and figure out why they're important. For him to hear me, I have to distill what I have to say and then give him the condensed version. I have to state my case in his language—which means it's best if I give him only three points and it's even better if they all start with the same letter.

What's more, when I'm presenting a problem, I try to tell him up front what I want him to do about it. If I just want a listening ear, I say so right away. Otherwise he'll spend the entire conversation coming up with solutions. Men are all about fixing things. That's what they do. So if you're appealing to a man—husband, boss, pastor, or friend—it's wise to make your expectations clear.

That's what Esther did. In two sentences, she told the king what the problem was and how he could solve it for her. She said, in essence, "My people and I have been sentenced to death. I'm asking you to spare our lives." And she got the best possible response.

> KING AHASUERUS ANSWERED AND SAID TO QUEEN ESTHER, "WHO IS HE, AND WHERE IS HE, WHO WOULD DARE PRESUME IN HIS HEART TO DO SUCH A THING?" AND ESTHER SAID, "THE ADVERSARY AND ENEMY IS THIS WICKED HAMAN!" SO HAMAN WAS TERRIFIED BEFORE THE KING AND QUEEN. THEN ... THEY HANGED HAMAN ON THE GALLOWS.
> (VV. 5-7, 10A)

Once Haman was dead, the king issued a new decree calling for the Jews to take up arms, destroy anyone who hated them, and plunder their houses. "And in every province and city, wherever the king's command and decree came, the Jews had joy and gladness, a feast and a holiday. Then many of the people of the land became Jews, because fear of the Jews fell upon them" (Esther 8:17).

What a great outcome! I love it, don't you? It's wonderful when appeals bring about the exact result we want. It's great when the kings in our lives make the right decision.

But that's not always what happens. Sometimes (in situations less dire than Esther's) our authorities make decisions we think are wrong. What should we do in such instances? Unless the decision is sinful in some way, once it's made, we should submit and support it.

A husband, especially, needs his wife to support his decisions. He depends on her to affirm his ability to lead. He wants to know she believes in him and trusts God to show him the right thing to do. Sometimes a man whose wife fails to express such confidence in him is afraid to be a leader not just at home but at work too. He's afraid to go after a job promotion or start a new business because he figures if his wife doesn't believe in him enough to follow his leadership, no one else will either.

Wives, please believe me when I say this: Submission builds men.

I'm convinced Robert is the leader he is today in part because 31 years ago I made up my mind to submit to him—even when he made mistakes. And, yes, along the way he has made some mistakes. We all do. But I chose as a young wife to treat his decisions—right or wrong—as if they were mine too. Sometimes I had to suffer in gracious silence through some unpleasant consequences as a result; but even so, I did my best to stick by him. I didn't go tell my friends or my parents about the bad decision he made. No, I covered him, and as I did I saw him learn from every mistake. I saw him grow day by day into a stronger leader.

"But what if my husband has a bad track record where decision making is concerned?" you might ask.

Then pray for him. A woman who submits to her husband can storm heaven with great faith and God will move on him in powerful ways just for her benefit. I tell you this not only because the Bible says so but because I've seen it happen.

Years ago when Robert was a bit rougher around the edges, making decisions I didn't approve of and ignoring my appeals, I spent a lot of time praying for his heart to be turned in the right direction. And God answered in ways that sometimes surprised me. He fought battles on my behalf I wouldn't have expected Him to even care about.

One in particular stands out in my mind: Robert had been away from home on a ministry trip for several weeks. The kids and I had planned a day of family fun so we could reconnect with each other when he returned. Robert knew about the plan and promised to set aside the day to spend with us.

Right after he got home from the airport, however, a friend called and asked him to play golf—at a very nice country club. We didn't have much money to spend on golf back then and since the friend had offered to pay for him, it seemed (to Robert, anyway) like an offer too good to refuse. So he asked me how I'd feel if he accepted.

"Well, we were really looking forward to our family day together, so we'll be disappointed," I said. Then, breathing a silent prayer for the grace to be nice about it, I added, "But if you want to play golf, it's okay. Go ahead."

Lest you think me too Edith Bunkerish, I assure you this was no spineless surrender. I've just learned over the years that I have to choose my battles. I can't afford to make big deals over little upsets. I must save my voice for the essential issues if I want to maximize my influence. When I see destructive patterns emerging or sense a certain course of action will violate a core value in our family, I'll say something about it; I'll energetically appeal.

But in this case, I didn't feel I should do so. Robert doesn't have a habit of disappointing our family. He's a loving, attentive husband and father. His desire to play golf was just a matter of personal preference. Since it wasn't wrong and it wouldn't cause any real harm, I decided to maintain harmony in our home and hold my peace. So I kept quiet.

God, on the other hand, did not. As Robert confessed to me later, when he headed out the door with his golf clubs, he heard the Lord say, "Don't go."

For once, obedient Robert wasn't. "I'm going to play golf, God," he answered. "Debbie said it was okay."

Driving to the country club, he noticed a headache coming on. It grew worse by the mile, so he stopped at a gas station and bought some aspirin. Gulping a couple of tablets, he got back in the car and continued on—head pounding—determined to play golf. By the time he and his friend teed off, in addition to the headache, nausea had to set in. On the first green, right there in front of his friend and the other country clubbers, he hit the breaking point ... and threw up.

"Okay, God, You win," he said, dragging his clubs back to the car.

As he drove back home, God gave him his instructions. "Tell Debbie you shouldn't have gone golfing. Repent to her, and I'll heal you."

"I have a headache! I don't want to tell her I'm sorry," he argued.

In the end, of course, Robert listened to the Lord. He came home, repented, God healed his head, and our family spent a great afternoon together. My husband learned a good lesson; things worked out for my benefit without me having to throw a fit or act ugly; and one more time I thanked the Lord—and Esther—for teaching me what submission can do.

CHAPTER 8

LEAVING THE
BAGGAGE BEHIND

*Suddenly Miriam became leprous, as white as snow ... So Miriam
was shut out of the camp seven days, and the people did not journey
till Miriam was brought in again.*

NUMBERS 12:10, 15

T HE DAY I STARTED SCHOOL, my first grade teacher
declared war on the great state of Texas. It was purely
an academic war, of course. No bullets flew. No bombs
exploded. But there were casualties just the same. And on a warm
September morning, as I curled my fingers around a crayon and
began to draw, I became one of them.

My teacher, by giving me a blank sheet of manila paper instead
of a reading primer, had fired her first shot.

To be clear, she wasn't really aiming at me. Her sites were set on
a recent Texas law that required all children five years old to enroll
in school—including the youngest of the bunch whose birthdays

fell in August. According to my teacher, August babies were still too immature for first grade. They had no hope of learning to read at such an early age. Therefore, the law should be changed. And she meant to prove it.

Thus, while the other children practiced the alphabet and stumbled through the adventures of Dick and Jane, she marched August-babies like me to a drawing table so we could color, remain illiterate, and make her point to the school board.

I don't think the school board noticed, but my mother did. Halfway through the year she saw I wasn't learning to read and tried to intervene. She asked the teacher first, then the principal, to provide the help I needed. But the principal happened to be the teacher's husband and an ally in the war on Texas, so their efforts to assist me were halfhearted at best.

At the end of the year, I was promoted to second grade without being tested ... and without being able to read. My parents and teachers failed to identify the problem and attributed my scholastic struggles over the next few years to a learning disability. The doctor prescribed Ritalin. The school prescribed special education classes.

Apparently, I just wasn't very smart.

At least that's what everybody thought. Everybody except God, that is. Unimpressed by other people's opinions and my own insecurity, He didn't see me as intellectually inferior. He believed I could learn just fine. So when I got saved as a fifth grader during an evangelistic revival at our church, He put a hunger in me to know what was in the Bible. Then He taught me how to read.

To this day, I don't know exactly what process He used. I never learned to sound out words phonetically like my children did when they were in school. I never had a tutor to help me catch up on the lessons I missed in first grade. But with the Bible as my textbook,

I somehow deciphered the hieroglyphics that had baffled me for years. I became a decent reader and began to do better in school—although I often lost points on my English compositions for using King James spellings.

I wish I could say my insecurity vanished with my illiteracy. But it didn't. Even without the help of my first grade teacher, my August-baby sense of inferiority lived on. And, like every other human being on the planet, I've been wrestling with insecurity in one way or another ever since.

The upside is, I've made some encouraging progress and I intend to win this wrestling match if it takes the rest of my life. I'm not going to do it like Miriam did either. Her insecurity earned her a seven-day time out and a week's worth of leprosy. Although she eventually learned her lesson, by studying her example I'm learning mine an easier way.

UPSTAGED BY MOSES

For a woman in Old Testament times, the Bible gives Miriam a lot of print. A major player in one of Scripture's greatest dramas, she had a myriad of reasons to feel secure about her place in the plan of God. But one thing bothered her. She was perpetually upstaged by her little brother. No matter how well she played her part, Moses always wound up in the spotlight.

She didn't mind it in the beginning when he was just a wriggling, cooing infant. Like most big sisters, Miriam thought Moses was marvelous back then. Born in Egypt at a time when Hebrew boys were being slaughtered, he needed her and she relished being there for him. She risked her life helping her parents hide him from Pharaoh's baby-killers. When he grew too big to conceal, she worked alongside her mother turning a bulrush basket into a water-proof cradle.

The day the family put Moses into the river—and into the hands of God—Miriam felt no twinge of sibling rivalry. Quite the opposite. Her eyes glistened with tears as she kissed her tiny brother's silken cheek and said goodbye. Her heart ached as her mother and father set his miniature ark afloat and watched it drift away on the waters of the fearsome Nile.

Although they'd all asked Jehovah to guide him to his divine destiny, Miriam couldn't bear to let Moses out of her sight that day. Running along the shore, she tracked his little boat as it bobbed among the reeds. She thought perhaps she could scare away the snakes that might try to crawl into it or—by sheer force of her faith—keep it in the shallows and out of the deep currents that could easily overturn it.

Even if she couldn't, at the very least she would see what happened next. She could bring back news to her heartbroken parents. Good or bad, they would want to know.

Of all the dangers that threatened baby Moses, the one Miriam didn't anticipate was Pharaoh's daughter. When her royal highness showed up with her servants at the river to bathe, Miriam caught her breath and took cover. Then she prayed. The basket was floating right toward the royal entourage. Only God could save little Moses now.

And sure enough, He did.

Pharaoh's daughter, spotting the curious craft, sent one of her maids to get it. "And when she opened it, she saw the child, and behold, the baby wept. So she had compassion on him, and said, 'This is one of the Hebrews' children'" (Exodus 2:6).

Suddenly, it was Miriam's moment to shine—and shine she did. Stepping out from her hiding place, she surprised Pharaoh's daughter with a brilliant idea: "Shall I go and call a nurse for you from the

Hebrew women, that she may nurse the child for you?" she asked.

> And Pharaoh's daughter said to her, "Go."
> So the maiden went and called the child's
> mother. Then Pharaoh's daughter said to her,
> "Take this child away and nurse him for me,
> and I will give you your wages." So the woman
> took the child and nursed him. (vv. 7-9)

Miriam knew even as the events unfolded that God had directed her steps and given her wisdom. The Almighty Himself had awarded her a role in saving Moses and it was a role she thoroughly enjoyed. Over the next few years, as her brother grew from infant to toddler, Miriam cherished the responsibilities and the subtle sense of superiority that comes with being an older sister. She may have complained about little Moses' mischievousness and his messes, but she smiled all the while.

Then one day everything changed.

Pharaoh's daughter whisked Moses away to the palace where he lived a lifestyle of royal privilege. Miriam stayed home and slogged through her days as a slave. He got an education while she baked bread and made bricks. He dressed in silk while she went ragged.

Somewhere along the way, she began to feel inferior, and insecurity set in.

After Moses grew up and ran away to Midian, Miriam may have put those insecurities behind her. But if she did, they resurfaced. For good reason. When her little brother returned from his 40-year hiatus on the backside of the desert, he made his entrance, not just as her parents' favorite child or a hot-shot royal prince, but as the miracle-working, prophet of God leading the Israelites to freedom.

Who can compete with that?

Miriam certainly couldn't. Or so it seemed to her. Never mind that God's hand was still on her life. Never mind that she was an acknowledged prophetess. Moses—the same kid who'd pulled her hair and stuck out his tongue at her when they were growing up—had stolen center stage; she was standing in his shadow, and she wasn't sure she mattered anymore.

So she did what we all tend to do when insecurity starts to drive us: She went on the attack. Drawing her other brother, Aaron, into the fray:

> MIRIAM AND AARON BEGAN TO TALK AGAINST MOSES BECAUSE OF HIS CUSHITE WIFE, FOR HE HAD MARRIED A CUSHITE. "HAS THE LORD SPOKEN ONLY THROUGH MOSES?" THEY ASKED. "HASN'T HE ALSO SPOKEN THROUGH US?" AND THE LORD HEARD THIS. (NUMBERS 12:1-2 NIV)

Here's a word to the wise. Comparing yourself to somebody else never works to your advantage. It either leaves you feeling superior and full of pride, or feeling inferior and full of envy. Either way, it's going to irritate God. Especially if the person to whom you're comparing yourself is one of His own.

Miriam can verify it. Her words of criticism and comparison had barely escaped her lips when …

> SUDDENLY THE LORD SAID TO MOSES, AARON, AND MIRIAM, "COME OUT, YOU THREE, TO THE TABERNACLE OF MEETING!" SO THE THREE CAME OUT. THEN THE LORD CAME DOWN IN THE PILLAR OF CLOUD

AND STOOD IN THE DOOR OF THE TABERNACLE, AND
CALLED AARON AND MIRIAM. AND THEY BOTH
WENT FORWARD. THEN HE SAID, "HEAR NOW MY
WORDS: IF THERE IS A PROPHET AMONG YOU, I, THE
LORD, MAKE MYSELF KNOWN TO HIM IN A VISION;
I SPEAK TO HIM IN A DREAM. NOT SO WITH MY
SERVANT MOSES; HE IS FAITHFUL IN ALL MY HOUSE.
I SPEAK WITH HIM FACE TO FACE, EVEN PLAINLY, AND
NOT IN DARK SAYINGS; AND HE SEES THE FORM OF
THE LORD. WHY THEN WERE YOU NOT AFRAID TO
SPEAK AGAINST MY SERVANT MOSES?" SO THE ANGER
OF THE LORD WAS AROUSED AGAINST THEM, AND
HE DEPARTED. AND WHEN THE CLOUD DEPARTED
FROM ABOVE THE TABERNACLE, SUDDENLY MIRIAM
BECAME LEPROUS, AS WHITE AS SNOW. THEN AARON
TURNED TOWARD MIRIAM, AND THERE SHE WAS, A
LEPER ... SO MIRIAM WAS SHUT OUT OF THE CAMP
SEVEN DAYS, AND THE PEOPLE DID NOT JOURNEY TILL
MIRIAM WAS BROUGHT IN AGAIN. (VV. 4-10, 15)

THE GHOST OF CHRISTMAS PAST

I'm eternally grateful to be a New Covenant believer living in the
dispensation of God's mercy and grace. Otherwise, I might have to
spend a week or two with leprosy myself because there have been
times in my life when I've been every bit as insecure as Miriam was.

ACCORDING TO ONE AUTHOR'S DESCRIPTION:

Insecurity refers to a profound sense of self-doubt—a
deep feeling of uncertainty about our basic worth and
our place in the world. Insecurity is associated with

chronic self-consciousness, along with a chronic lack of confidence in ourselves and anxiety about our relationships. The insecure man or woman lives in constant fear of rejection and a deep uncertainty about whether his or her own feelings and desires are legitimate. [1]

I can add an "amen" to that definition and provide any number of personal illustrations. I don't have a little brother named Moses to blame for them either. Nor can I give all the credit to my first grade teacher. The fact is, I contracted a massive case of insecurity pretty much on my own. I didn't need anybody to upstage me. I down-staged myself (if there is such a thing) so painfully and at such a young age that I vowed early in life never to get on stage at all—ever again.

The catastrophes began with my third grade Christmas pageant. Standing on the first row of risers in the new dress my mother had made me with my hair in uncharacteristic curls, I humiliated myself. Right there in front my parents, my schoolmates, and everybody else, I butchered the one line I'd been given. One simple line. About Jesus. And I messed it up so horrifically, no one had a clue what I said.

The pageant proceeded despite my blunder, of course. Most likely, nobody paid much attention to it. But the incident left an indelible tattoo on my brain, a permanent reminder of what a poor public communicator I am.

In high school, I once tried to prove the tattoo wrong. As an officer in a scholastic club, I agreed to memorize yet another line and deliver it at an installation ceremony. But history repeated itself. I got so tangled up in the sentence it's a wonder they didn't have to bring in the Jaws of Life to cut me out.

Afterwards, my mother insisted I take speech classes. I assured her I didn't need them because I would never, this side of the Millennial reign, set foot on a public platform again. Ignoring my protests, my mother prevailed and I ended up taking the classes. But they did nothing to allay my insecurity. Nor did they significantly improve my ability. When it came to public speaking, I appeared to be permanently impaired.

This did not hinder me, however, from marrying one of our generation's greatest communicators. Talk about upstaging yourself! I did it in a major way. Although the Lord clearly put Robert and me together it sometimes seemed like a practical joke. *Really, Lord?* I wondered. *You think I'm the best helpmate for him?*

Not that I ever wanted to compete with Robert. I was perfectly satisfied to work hard and support him behind the scenes. I'm a great back stage performer. I like to push other people out front. But as Robert's wife and a leader in ministry, I couldn't hide forever. Like the ghost of Christmas past, the specter of public speaking soon came knocking.

My reaction?

Stark terror.

My own deficiencies in themselves were enough to give me nightmares. When I added to them the fear that people would expect me to have the same gifting my husband has, my hair almost stood on end. Imagining how people would compare me to him and be disappointed, I rejected every invitation to speak.

God, however, refused to take no for an answer. So did the team at Gateway. They kept asking ... and asking ... and asking me to speak. Encouraging and persistent, they waited with patience for me to overcome my insecurity just like the Lord and the people of Israel waited for Miriam to recover from her leprosy—and they did it with great grace. Over time, I surrendered little by little to God's will. I accepted His definition of who I am (which is the one sure cure for insecurity) and began to step into the role He's given me to fill.

Although I'm still a work in progress, these days I find myself on a platform with a microphone more often than I ever expected. I'm not exactly comfortable with it yet. But I've decided it's okay with me for people to see who I really am—even if it's not what they want. I've accepted the place of leadership God has chosen for me, and I'm growing more confident day by day that, despite my many inadequacies, together God and I are able.

HIDING IN THE LUGGAGE OF LIFE

In addition to my aversion to leprosy, one of the reasons I'm so determined to drive insecurity out of my life is because I don't want to end up like King Saul. (He's a man, so he's not officially one of our mentors, but I've learned a lot from him anyway.) More hard-headed than Miriam, Saul didn't learn his lesson in a week and then move on. He let his insecurities fester for decades. Eventually they became lethal. But not until they'd produced four dangerous byproducts that will poison anyone who lets insecurity call the shots in their lives.

The first of those byproducts surfaced the day of Saul's coronation. It was a time when he seemed to have everything going for him: He'd been divinely called and anointed by the foremost prophet of the land to be the leader of the nation. His call had been confirmed by three supernatural signs. God had given him a new heart to equip him for his position. And if that wasn't enough, he was strikingly handsome and a head taller than any other man in the land.

What more could anyone need to feel secure? Saul had it all! Yet when the moment came for him to be presented to the people as their king and "they looked for him, he was not to be found. So they inquired further of the LORD, 'Has the man come here yet?' And the LORD said, 'Yes, he has hidden himself among the baggage'" (1 Samuel 10:21-22, NIV).

You have to admit, it was a strange way for a national leader to behave. Imagine an inauguration postponed because the president-elect is hiding in the trunk of somebody's car and you get the picture. It's insecurity on steroids and Saul suffered from it because he didn't believe what God said about him. He believed his feelings of inadequacy instead. Rather than seeing Himself through God's eyes as the divinely chosen head of the tribes of Israel, he saw himself as the least among those tribes (1 Samuel 9:21, 15:17).

We all know what that's like. We've done it. We've looked in the Bible, seen the wonderful things God said about us, and then let our past insecurities override them. We've heard the Lord calling us to step out in faith and listened to the voice of our doubts instead.

In other words, we've all spent time hanging out with the baggage.

And why not? Baggage can actually be quite companionable. It doesn't expect anything of us. It won't judge us for our mistakes. But then, it won't applaud us for our victories either.

Maybe that's why David didn't spend much time with it. The exact opposite of Saul, he had no patience with the luggage of life. Although he had plenty of excuses to feel insecure, young David had such confidence in God that when he visited his big brothers on the battlefield and saw the Israeli and Philistine armies facing each other, he "left his luggage with a baggage officer and hurried out to the ranks" (1 Samuel 17:22, TLB).

Then, while insecure Saul shivered in his tent unable to believe God because of his insecurity, David killed Goliath.

The baggage didn't say anything about David's triumph. But everybody else sure did. They've been talking about it ever since.

You and I can either choose to be like Saul or like David. We can hide out in the insecurities of our past; or we can decide to believe what God says about us, put our confidence in Him, and leave the baggage behind us where it really belongs.

INSECURE LEADERS MAKE IRRATIONAL DECISIONS

Not only does insecurity result in an inability to believe God, it causes people to make impetuous and even irrational decisions. It tricks us into doing stupid stuff. Saul demonstrated it over and over again.

Take for example the time he declared a fast and forced his army to go without food right in the middle of a battle with the Philistines. I'm no military expert but even I can figure out that's a dumb idea. Soldiers weakened from hunger fighting a well-fed foe are at a definite disadvantage. Yet Saul ignored this obvious fact. He was so insecure in his place with God that, abandoning all wisdom and compassion for his men, he resorted to religious gamesmanship. He tried to earn God's favor (and a military victory) by impressing Him with a legalistic sacrifice.

> Now the men of Israel were in distress that day, because Saul had bound the people under an oath, saying, "Cursed be any man who eats food before evening comes, before I have avenged myself on my enemies!" So none of the troops tasted food. The entire army entered the woods, and there was honey on the ground. When they went into the woods, they saw the honey oozing out, yet no one put his hand to his mouth, because they feared the oath. (1 SAMUEL 14:24-26, NIV)

You have to wonder what on earth Saul was thinking in this situation. Why was he so stubbornly determined to make his troops maintain the fast? Didn't he realize he already had God's favor upon him? Didn't Saul know God had made him Israel's commander (1 Samuel 10:1) and would therefore freely give him the victory he was trying in his own strength to attain?

No, he didn't.

That was the whole problem. Saul never truly trusted God's call on his life. He was always trying to become what he already was. He felt unworthy to be king so he was constantly trying to prove himself. But it was a hopeless quest. None of us qualify for what God has called us to do. He doesn't even ask us to. He simply asks us to acknowledge His grace and pursue a relationship with Him. All He requires is that we give Him our heart, surrender ourselves to His will, and inquire of Him, "Lord, what do You want me to do?"

My responsibilities don't compare to Saul's, so I can't identify with the struggles he faced, but I do know what it's like to feel unworthy of God's call. When I think about what He is doing through Gateway, I don't understand why He's chosen me to be a leader here. In myself, I'm totally unqualified. Yet I know I'm in God's hand, and the more secure I become in my relationship with Him, the more secure I am in the position I've been given.

Because I accept this plan as God's and not mine, I don't have to worry that somehow I cheated the system and ended up here by accident. I can be confident the Lord Himself has given me this little corner of the world to inhabit and He will enable me to make a difference here. He will empower me to bless this place and these people with His love.

God's love is the bottom line, after all. As leaders—at home, at work, or at church—the most godly thing we can do is care for people. If we're so insecure we feel we must impress them, or even impress the Lord, with our super-spirituality we're going to harm our own cause, erode our authority, and lose the confidence of those we're supposed to be leading.

Which is exactly what happened to Saul. When his son Jonathan caught up with his father's troops, he hadn't heard about the fasting command:

> So he reached out the end of the staff that was in his hand and dipped it into the honeycomb. He raised his hand to his mouth, and his eyes brightened. Then one of the soldiers told him, "Your father bound the army under a strict oath, saying, 'Cursed be any man who eats food today!' That is why the men are faint." Jonathan said, "My father has made trouble for the country. See how my eyes brightened when I tasted a little of this honey. How much better it would have been if the men had eaten today some of the plunder they took from their enemies. Would not the slaughter of the Philistines have been even greater?" (1 Samuel 14:27-30, NIV)

Actually, Jonathan just said out loud what everybody else (except Saul) must have been thinking. He acknowledged the irrationality of his father's decision and admitted it had cost the Israelites an even greater victory.

Most likely, Saul's soldiers never fully trusted his leadership again. Why should they? This wasn't a one-time mistake. Saul routinely undermined his own leadership with such disastrous decisions. Even worse than the fasting debacle was the decision he made in a fit of anger when David—whom he was trying to kill at the time— slipped away from him. Threatened by David's military success and popularity, Saul vented his fury on the innocent people he blamed for David's escape and said:

> "HEAR NOW, YOU BENJAMITES! ... ALL OF YOU HAVE CONSPIRED AGAINST ME, AND THERE IS NO ONE WHO REVEALS TO ME THAT MY SON HAS MADE A COVENANT WITH THE SON OF JESSE; AND THERE IS NOT ONE OF YOU WHO IS SORRY FOR ME OR REVEALS TO ME THAT MY SON HAS STIRRED UP MY SERVANT AGAINST ME, TO LIE IN WAIT, AS IT IS THIS DAY." THEN ANSWERED DOEG THE EDOMITE, WHO WAS SET OVER THE SERVANTS OF SAUL, AND SAID, "I SAW [DAVID] THE SON OF JESSE GOING TO NOB, TO AHIMELECH THE SON OF AHITUB. AND HE INQUIRED OF THE LORD FOR HIM, GAVE HIM PROVISIONS, AND GAVE HIM THE SWORD OF GOLIATH THE PHILIS-TINE." (1 SAMUEL 22:7-10)

Did you notice the name of the man who spoke to Saul there? It's *Doeg*, which in Hebrew is derived from the root word for *fear*. That's significant because fear and insecurity are close cousins. Fear speaks to our insecurities like Doeg spoke to the king. It provokes us to make decisions we'll regret, decisions that will not only hurt us but others as well.

Because Saul listened to Doeg's accusations he believed the innocent priest Ahimelech had betrayed him by assisting David. In a paranoid rage, he cast aside all reverence for the Lord and commanded his guards to kill not just Ahimelech but the other priests as well. When the guards refused, he ordered Doeg to do it. "So Doeg turned on them and killed them, eighty-five priests in all, all wearing their priestly robes" (v. 18, TLB).

This is serious business. Old Testament priests were God's representatives who heard and relayed His voice to the people. Yet Saul recklessly decided to have them murdered. In doing so, he portrayed a spiritual truth as relevant to us today as it was to Saul: the combination of fear and insecurity will kill the voice of God in our lives.

I've seen it happen. I once watched a woman in church leadership self destruct right before my eyes because of insecurity. Fear got her ear and pushed her to make poor decisions. Frantic to protect her place of authority, she acted impetuously and irrationally. She was a gifted woman, but she ultimately lost the respect of everyone around her and her position of leadership as well.

INSTABILITY AND INSANE JEALOUSY

As if his inability to believe and his impetuous decisions weren't bad enough, Saul also became famous for the instability of his soul. He routinely swung from the heights of glory to the depths of despair. First the Spirit of the Lord was upon him; then an evil spirit tormented him (1 Samuel 16:14). One moment he was trying to murder David; the next he was prophesying (1 Samuel 19:23).

Insecurity and instability form a vicious cycle. They feed one another. When we're insecure, we try to regain our security by controlling things. Then we realize we can't do it and we become anxious and upset again. It's like an emotional seesaw: we're up if things are going our way, and we're down when they're not.

Such instability doesn't belong in the lives of believers. On the contrary, the Bible says, "The root of the righteous will never be moved" (Proverbs 12:3, ESV).

Secure, stable Christians are such a blessing. I love to be around them! I don't have to wonder what kind of mood they'll be in from one moment to the next. They're like Jesus—the same yesterday, today, and forever (Hebrews 13:8). Because they believe God is in control, they don't try to be. They just carry out their responsibilities the best they can and if things don't work out as planned, they trust the Lord and roll with whatever comes their way.

As grace-filled, life-giving women, that's how we should aim to be. And we can do it if we'll deal with our insecurities.

Do you know what else we can do?

We can conquer one of the most hazardous by-products of all: the green-eyed monster of jealousy. That's something Saul never did. He let jealousy latch onto him the day he heard the people celebrating David's triumph over Goliath.

THIS WAS THEIR SONG: "SAUL HAS SLAIN HIS THOU-
SANDS, AND DAVID HIS TEN THOUSANDS!" OF
COURSE SAUL WAS VERY ANGRY. "WHAT'S THIS?" HE
SAID TO HIMSELF. "THEY CREDIT DAVID WITH TEN
THOUSANDS AND ME WITH ONLY THOUSANDS. NEXT
THEY'LL BE MAKING HIM THEIR KING!" SO FROM
THAT TIME ON KING SAUL KEPT A JEALOUS WATCH
ON DAVID. (1 SAMUEL 18:7-9, TLB)

Saul's "jealous watch" soon mushroomed into a murderous obsession that corrupted his character and consumed his life. He became David's enemy continually (v. 28) and devoted years to destroying him. After failing to accomplish his goal, Saul died an insanely jealous man.

Although it's an Old Testament story, it's not an Old Testament problem. The New Testament still warns us to beware of "bitter jealousy and selfish ambition ... For where jealousy and selfish ambition exist, there will be disorder and every vile practice" (James 3:14, 16, ESV).

Some things never change and this is one of them: Insecurity unchecked turns into sin. It results in an inability to believe, impetuous and irrational decisions, instability of soul, and even insane jealousy. It leaves leaders like Miriam sitting on the sidelines and makes kings like Saul unfit to reign.

So let's kick insecurity to the curb. Let's believe what God says about us and see ourselves as He sees us. Instead of fretting about our deficiencies, let's focus on His sufficiency and have the time of our lives making a difference in our little corner of the world.

PUTTING FIRST
THINGS FIRST

Honor the LORD with your possessions, and with the firstfruits of all
your increase; so your barns will be filled with plenty, and your vats will
overflow with new wine.

PROVERBS 3:9-10

G OD DOESN'T THINK LIKE MOST PEOPLE DO—which is why Elijah wasn't shocked when he saw the stick-gathering widow he'd been sent to find. Sunken-cheeked and stomach growling, threadbare and trailed by a son as skinny as a scarecrow, she seemed an unlikely benefactor. But Elijah knew right away she was the one.

The Lord had described her to him when the ravens stopped delivering his dinners and the Brook Cherith dried up: "Arise, go to Zarephath, which belongs to Sidon, and dwell there," He'd said. "See, I have commanded a widow there to provide for you" (1 Kings 17:9).

If Elijah had been an average kind of guy, he wouldn't have

recognized her. He would have been looking for a woman of wealth and distinction. He would have been expecting someone with something to give, not a starving, penniless waif with a need to receive.

But Elijah was well-acquainted with the way God operates. He knew that even in the midst of a nation-wide famine and drought, the Almighty could supply food in a dozen different ways. He could order up another batch of birds to deliver take-out. He could turn stones into bread or rain manna from heaven. The fact that He'd chosen a person to provide for Elijah's needs could only mean one thing.

He'd found somebody to bless.

That's why the famous prophet didn't flinch when he discovered his ministry's sole supporter scrounging for firewood and planning her final meal. Unflustered by her obvious poverty, he simply set God's strategy in motion. He asked her to bring him a cup of water and a morsel of bread.

Considering Elijah's reputation, it must have seemed like a peculiar request. He was, after all, renowned throughout the region for his divine wisdom. His God-given perception was so sharp most people called him a Seer. So the widow must have been startled by his cluelessness. Staring at him in astonishment she must have wondered, *Can't this Seer see I'm in no position to offer him hospitality?*

Apparently he couldn't, so she helped him out and straightforwardly informed him of her situation.

"As the LORD your God lives, I do not have bread, only a handful of flour in a bin, and a little oil in a jar; and see, I am gathering a couple of sticks that I may go in and prepare it for myself and my son, that we may eat

IT, AND DIE." AND ELIJAH SAID TO HER, "DO NOT
FEAR; GO AND DO AS YOU HAVE SAID, BUT MAKE ME
A SMALL CAKE FROM IT FIRST, AND BRING IT TO ME;
AND AFTERWARD MAKE SOME FOR YOURSELF AND
YOUR SON. FOR THUS SAYS THE LORD GOD OF ISRA-
EL: 'THE BIN OF FLOUR SHALL NOT BE USED UP, NOR
SHALL THE JAR OF OIL RUN DRY, UNTIL THE DAY THE
LORD SENDS RAIN ON THE EARTH.'" (VV. 12-14)

It's natural to assume when reading this story that God sent the widow to take care of Elijah. But actually, the opposite is true. God sent Elijah to take care of the widow. By asking her to feed His prophet, He connected her with His limitless resources. He provided her the opportunity to give to Him first so He could reciprocate and give to her abundantly in return.

SO SHE WENT AWAY AND DID ACCORDING TO THE
WORD OF ELIJAH; AND SHE AND HE AND HER HOUSE-
HOLD ATE FOR MANY DAYS. THE BIN OF FLOUR WAS
NOT USED UP, NOR DID THE JAR OF OIL RUN DRY, AC-
CORDING TO THE WORD OF THE LORD WHICH HE
SPOKE BY ELIJAH. (VV. 15-16)

You can't outgive God. The widow can confirm it. She believed His promise, gave Him a little, and He rewarded her with a lot. She put Him first and He multiplied her groceries and made them last.

Why did He do it?

Because it's His nature. He is a giving God!

He doesn't just give money, either. Whenever someone puts Him first in their life, He blesses them in countless ways. He provides benefits too precious for money to buy. The widow can confirm that too.

God orchestrated her circumstances and saved her son's life—not just once but twice. First, he spared him from starvation with the bottomless bin of flour and unending supply of oil. Then He worked a second miracle. He arranged for Elijah to be on hand when the boy fell sick and died.

With a prophet as her houseguest, the boy's mother knew exactly what to do the day the tragedy struck. She turned to Elijah for help. He took the boy to the upper room of her house where he was staying:

> AND HE STRETCHED HIMSELF OUT ON THE CHILD THREE TIMES, AND CRIED OUT TO THE LORD AND SAID, "O LORD MY GOD, I PRAY, LET THIS CHILD'S SOUL COME BACK TO HIM." THEN THE LORD HEARD THE VOICE OF ELIJAH; AND THE SOUL OF THE CHILD CAME BACK TO HIM, AND HE REVIVED. AND ELIJAH TOOK THE CHILD AND BROUGHT HIM DOWN FROM THE UPPER ROOM INTO THE HOUSE, AND GAVE HIM TO HIS MOTHER. AND ELIJAH SAID, "SEE, YOUR SON LIVES!" (VV. 21-23)

Jesus taught that those who receive a prophet will receive a prophet's reward, and those who give a disciple so much as a cup of cold water will by no means lose that reward (Matthew 10:41-42). Elijah's widow showed us how it's done. She not only gave to the prophet—and thus, to the Lord—in her most desperate hour of need, she gave to Him *first*. And in return for a gift so small it could be valued in pennies, He returned to her the priceless gift of her only son.

THE PIZZA PLACE BLESSING

When Robert and I started our journey of extravagant giving, the nation was not in famine. We were in no danger of starving and we knew it. So I don't want to suggest we've ever walked a mile (or even a block) in the shoes of the woman from Zarephath. But I do think the look on Robert's face might have resembled the shock Elijah witnessed when he asked the widow to give him some cake.

After all, on the night our adventure began, Robert wasn't accustomed to giving away our entire month's income ... and that's exactly what the Lord asked him to do.

Panicked, he initially hoped he'd somehow misunderstood the instructions. Staring longingly at the check he'd just received, he couldn't imagine God would ask him to part with it so soon. A love offering from a church, the pastor had presented it to him only moments before. "I'm pleased and amazed to tell you this is the largest love offering this little church has ever given," he'd said. "God used you to bless us tonight, and I'm so happy to be able to give this to you."

As a traveling evangelist, Robert counted on such offerings to pay our bills. This was the only church he was scheduled to preach in all month. Normally he ministered several times a month and still brought home just enough to provide for our household. But when he looked at the amount on the check, he realized God had done the miraculous: with one offering He'd completely covered our monthly expenses.

Now, after basking briefly in the wonder of God's amazing provision, Robert was scrambling to figure out how we'd get by if he gave the offering away.

Lord, this can't be Your voice! he argued. *You've just done a miracle here to meet our needs!*

God responded by simply repeating His instructions. Drawing Robert's attention to a missionary standing on the other side of the empty sanctuary, He said, *Give him the whole offering. Trust me.*

Usually quick to obey, Robert found himself resisting the Lord's leading. He gripped the check tighter and prayed that God would change His mind.

I've heard Robert tell the story innumerable times: "I tried to rationalize. I tried bargaining. I tried begging," he says. "But the impression only grew stronger. Ultimately, I waved the white flag. I endorsed the back of the check, folded it in half and took a quick glance around the room to make sure no one was watching. Walking up to the missionary, I said something like, 'I really appreciated your testimony tonight. Please, don't tell anyone about this, but I would like you to have this offering. The check is made out to me, but I have signed it over to you.' I handed him the check and walked away."

Because we were tithers, Robert and I already knew about putting God first in our finances. We'd learned some things about how to trust God with our money. But this kind of giving required a whole new level of faith. It also opened the door to a new level of blessing.

An hour later, we found that out. Sitting in a pizza place after the service with some couples from the church, a man Robert hardly knew leaned across the table and asked him a startling question. "How much was your offering tonight?" Robert, too stunned by the man's audacity to figure out what else to do, told him. Then the man asked an even more brazen question. "Where is the check?"

Reluctant to reveal that he'd given it away, Robert lied. (Can you believe it?!) He said he'd given the check to me. When the man asked to see it, Robert pretended to make an effort to retrieve it. He got up, went to the end of the table where I was sitting, and whispered to me, "How's your pizza?" After I looked quizzically at him and said my pizza was fine, he returned to his chair and—yes!—he lied again. He told the man I'd put the check in the car.

"The check's not in the car, Robert," he replied.

"How do you know that?"

"Because God told me—and He told me something else." Unfolding a check made out for exactly 10 times the amount of the one Robert had given away, the man held it out and motioned for Robert to take it. As he did, instead of letting the check go, the man held onto it for a moment and looked Robert in the eye as they held the check between them. "God is about to teach you about giving so you can teach the Body of Christ," he said. Then he released the check.

Although I know for a fact the man with the check was not Elijah, he had just as much effect. His spiritual sensitivity and obedience helped set in motion the Lord's strategy in our lives. It helped launch us into a life of Spirit-led giving that would prove to us beyond any doubt that it's impossible to outgive God.

RAISING THE STAKES

During the next year and a half, we gave and received more extravagantly than we'd ever imagined. We gave away nine vehicles, and each time we gave one the Lord replaced it. We increased our giving to 70 percent and, because our income skyrocketed, we lived more comfortably on the 30 percent than we had on the 90.

As our faith and boldness grew, the Lord kept raising the stakes and showing us just how much He could do. Toward the end of those 18 months, He led us to give away all we owned: both of our cars, our house, and all the money in our bank accounts. We prayed about it long enough to be sure we'd heard correctly, sought the Lord about how and to whom we were to give, and then we obeyed.

Once again, God blessed us beyond measure in return.

Often people who hear about that season of our life ask how I felt about giving everything away. My response sometimes surprises them. They assume I had to struggle through fear or sadness. But I didn't. On the contrary, I was excited. We were on a God adventure! Like Peter walking on the water, we'd stepped out of the boat and fixed our eyes on Jesus, the author and finisher of our faith. Our giving didn't seem to me like some great sacrifice. It was just simple obedience to the Lord, and I felt joyful about it. Stuff, after all, is just stuff. It's not really important—especially compared to the incorruptible rewards of heaven.

Even if I'd had some negative emotions to deal with, it wouldn't have mattered. This wasn't about emotions, it was about obedience to God; and obeying Him at any level always gives us an opportunity to be blessed.

I didn't necessarily think God's blessing would make us wealthy, but I was confident we wouldn't wind up on the street. I never worried we'd be unable to pay our bills. Robert and I had trusted God and seen His faithfulness in our lives time and again. We knew He'd provide for us. We weren't novices blundering around on blind faith. We'd been on a God journey for years. This was just another step.

I also had the security of knowing my husband would work as many jobs as necessary to take care of me. He's always been diligent with our family's finances. Never in our marriage have I been concerned that we'd fail to meet our obligations. Our credit score is great. Robert is a giver, yes, but he also takes care of business.

There have been times when our income seemed enormous to me but, because we were also giving away an enormous amount, our lifestyle remained frugal. On occasion, the phenomenon mystified me. Robert would tell me about a great love offering we'd received and I'd say, "Yea! Now I can buy the new sofa I've been wanting!"

"No, we don't have the money for it," he'd answer.

"Why not? Where did it all go?" I was tempted to ask. But I knew how Robert managed things. Because we lived by faith, he would pay our house payment two or three months in advance. He'd put some money in savings. And He'd give however the Lord led. So, quite often, there wasn't any money left for splurges.

That was okay with me, though. I don't need a lot to be happy. I like nice things, so if I'm going to get them I want them to be good, but if necessary I can go without them. I care more about our family relationships, having quality ties with our kids and grandkids, than I do about stuff.

The only thing I resented a little during our special season of extravagant giving was that some people assumed we were rich. They'd hear we'd given a car to someone and they'd expect us to give them a car too. They didn't understand we could only do those kinds of things when God told us to. People also made comments about how we didn't know what it was like to be late on a payment. Granted, because of Robert's stewardship, we weren't late on any payments, but we definitely knew what it was like to have them. We stretched and budgeted our dollars just like everyone else.

Sometimes we skipped going out to eat. Sometimes we cut expenses in other ways. But even in the leanest times, we were blessed because we'd learned life's most vital lesson: Always, *always* put God first.

ANY FIRST THING GIVEN IS NEVER LOST

It's no accident that Elijah asked the widow to give him the first of her meager provisions. He didn't do it capriciously or just because he was heartless and hungry. Others might have thought so. They might have grumbled about Elijah's selfishness and said, "Shouldn't a compassionate man of God have made the widow's needs his priority? Shouldn't he have encouraged her to feed herself and her son first and then bring him the leftovers?"

But the answer to their questions would be no and here's why: God never asks for the leftovers. All through the Bible, He makes it clear that the first of everything belongs to Him. It's an unchanging spiritual principle. It can be called the principle of the firstborn, the firstfruits, or the tithe, but no matter what title we choose, it directly affects the measure of God's blessing we enjoy in our lives.

Robert's book, *The Blessed Life*, contains a wonderful and thorough teaching on this principle. In case you haven't yet read it, or need to be reminded, which we all do, I want to take a brief look at the Scriptures that show us just how important firsts are to the Lord.

Let's start with the principle of the firstborn. It initially appears in the fourth chapter of Genesis where Cain and Abel bring their offerings to the Lord. As the story goes:

> ABEL WAS A KEEPER OF SHEEP, BUT CAIN WAS A TILLER OF THE GROUND. AND IN THE PROCESS OF TIME IT CAME TO PASS THAT CAIN BROUGHT AN OFFERING OF THE FRUIT OF THE GROUND TO THE LORD. ABEL ALSO BROUGHT OF THE FIRSTBORN OF HIS FLOCK AND OF THEIR FAT. AND THE LORD RESPECTED ABEL AND HIS OFFERING, BUT HE DID NOT RESPECT CAIN AND HIS OFFERING.
> (GENESIS 4:2-5, EMPHASIS ADDED)

People are sometimes confused about God's rejection of Cain's offering. But the explanation is simple. Unlike Abel, who gave God the firstborn, which represented the first of his increase, Cain gave the leftovers. He grew his crops, reaped his harvest, took care of his own personal business and then "in the process of time," he got around to giving an offering.

According to God, such an attitude is dangerous. He said it indicates that "sin lies at the door" (v. 7). Like Cain, anyone who fails to put God first in their lives is headed for big trouble.

We find the principle of the firstborn mentioned again in Exodus 13. There, the Lord established an enduring spiritual precedent by making this command to the Israelites who were about to be freed from the slavery of Egypt:

> CONSECRATE TO ME ALL THE FIRSTBORN, WHAT-
> EVER OPENS THE WOMB AMONG THE CHILDREN OF
> ISRAEL, BOTH OF MAN AND BEAST; IT IS MINE ... SET
> APART TO THE LORD ALL THAT OPEN THE WOMB,
> THAT IS, EVERY FIRSTBORN THAT COMES FROM AN
> ANIMAL WHICH YOU HAVE; THE MALES SHALL BE THE
> LORD'S. BUT EVERY FIRSTBORN OF A DONKEY YOU
> SHALL REDEEM WITH A LAMB; AND IF YOU WILL NOT
> REDEEM IT, THEN YOU SHALL BREAK ITS NECK. AND
> ALL THE FIRSTBORN OF MAN AMONG YOUR SONS YOU
> SHALL REDEEM. (EXODUS 13:2, 12-13)

Notice those verses not only verify that the firstborn belongs to God, they reveal another crucial fact: under the Old Covenant, every firstborn had to be either sacrificed or redeemed by a lamb that took its place. Sacrifice or redemption—those were the only two choices. There was no third option.

How does that principle relate to us as New Covenant believers? We're the beneficiaries of it!

Jesus as The Lamb of God who takes away the sin of the world (John. 1:29) was sacrificed in our place. God gave His Firstborn so that we could be redeemed. What's more, He gave Him first—before we believed. Romans 5:8 says:

> GOD DEMONSTRATES HIS OWN LOVE TOWARD US, IN THAT WHILE WE WERE STILL SINNERS, CHRIST DIED FOR US.

God didn't wait to see if we would repent and turn to Him before He sent Jesus to the cross. He offered Jesus in advance, by faith. He gave to us the same way He asks us to give to Him—first, before we see the blessings that will follow.

If you've had the idea that the principle of giving God our firsts is just Old Testament business, read about how the Israelites carried out God's command on the night of the first Passover. Picture in your mind what happened: After sacrificing a lamb for each household, they dipped a hyssop branch in the blood. They applied it first on the left side of the door frame and then on the right side. Finally, they put the blood on top of the mantle in the middle so that it would drip down. In doing so, they created the form of the cross—and that cross saved them. When the plague swept through the land the Egyptians' firstborn, who by divine right belonged to God but had been withheld from Him, were killed. But the Israelites whose firstborn had been given to God and redeemed were spared.

What a perfect illustration of New Covenant salvation!

It's been said that any first thing given is never lost, and any first thing not given is always lost. What we give to God, we don't lose because God redeems it for us. But what we withhold from God, we will lose. The Egyptians found that out the hard way. But as believers we don't have to. We can learn from the Bible to give our first to the Lord.

GIVING THE FIRST REDEEMS THE REST

In addition to laying claim to the firstborn, God also reveals throughout the Bible that the first tenth of our financial increase belongs to Him. Patriarchs like Abraham and Jacob set the example and God explained it when the Israelites were preparing to take the Promised Land. He said simply, "The first of the firstfruits of your land you shall bring into the house of the LORD your God" (Exodus 23:19).

Notice, God wants the first of our firstfruits. He doesn't want us to write checks for our house payment and our car, buy a week's worth of groceries and a pair of shoes, and then give to Him. He wants the first check we write to be our tithe check.

"Well, I think that's silly," somebody might say. "Why would God care which part of my income He gets as long as I give Him ten percent?"

Because it's not just our money God wants, it's our faith. "Without faith it is impossible to please Him" (Hebrews 11:6), and there's not much faith involved in giving 10 percent to God after all your other expenses are met. What's more, it's not really putting God first when you pay everybody else and then see if there's enough left to give Him.

That's the reason God instructed the Israelites to give Him all the spoils from Jericho. It was the first city they conquered when they went into Canaan. If giving the first tenth wasn't important, God could have said, "Conquer 10 cities and give Me all the spoils from the tenth one." But He didn't. He essentially said, "Give Me the first and you can have the rest."

Obeying that command took an act of faith by the Israelites—which was the whole point. God knew they needed His blessing to take the Promised Land. They needed to have their priorities right and be walking by faith if they were going to win all the battles facing them. So—at a time when their future victories were yet to be won and when resources were at their lowest ebb—the Lord asked for their tithe.

Sadly, one Israelite disobeyed God's command. A man named Achan fell in love with "a beautiful Babylonian garment, two hundred shekels of silver, and a wedge of gold" he found in Jericho (Joshua 7:21). So he hid them in his tent. As a result, Israel suffered a humiliating defeat in their next battle and 36 of their men were killed.

What a tragedy! Israel would have been blessed in that battle if Achan's treasures had been consecrated to God as firstfruits. But because he withheld them, Israel was cursed.

The same is true for us. If we take for ourselves what belongs to God, we relinquish His blessing. We come under a curse because we're in possession of stolen goods.

I realize those are strong statements, but they mirror the message God delivered to the people who withheld their tithes in Malachi's day. He said to them:

> "WILL A MAN ROB GOD? YET YOU HAVE ROBBED ME!
> BUT YOU SAY, 'IN WHAT WAY HAVE WE ROBBED YOU?'
> IN TITHES AND OFFERINGS. YOU ARE CURSED WITH A
> CURSE, FOR YOU HAVE ROBBED ME, EVEN THIS WHOLE
> NATION. BRING ALL THE TITHES INTO THE STORE-
> HOUSE, THAT THERE MAY BE FOOD IN MY HOUSE,
> AND TRY ME NOW IN THIS ... IF I WILL NOT OPEN

FOR YOU THE WINDOWS OF HEAVEN AND POUR OUT
FOR YOU SUCH BLESSING THAT THERE WILL NOT BE
ROOM ENOUGH TO RECEIVE IT." (MALACHI 3:8-10)

The Bible leaves no doubt about it: The firstfruits, or the tithe, is the portion that redeems the rest. By giving it we put God first in our lives and release our faith, and faith is the trigger that initiates His blessings.

No wonder Proverbs 3:9-10 says, "Honor the LORD with your possessions, and with the firstfruits of all your increase; so your barns will be filled with plenty, and your vats will overflow with new wine."

STATION WAGONS, HAIRDRYERS, AND STEREO STANDS

To tell the whole truth, Robert and I don't just give the first tenth to God. We don't just give him offerings. We surrender everything we have to Him. Jesus is Lord of it all. So whatever He tells us to do with our money—or anything else for that matter—we do it.

Some years ago, for instance, the Lord dropped it in our hearts to rid ourselves of debt. That meant selling the nice car we'd been driving (which was financed) and replacing it with an old (and I mean Methuselah old!) station wagon. The thing drank a quart of oil a week and was capable of conking out on us at any time and leaving us stranded on the side of the road. It was definitely an adventure on wheels.

We also made a commitment to buy only what we could pay for with cash. So when my hairdryer broke and we didn't have an extra $20 to spend on a replacement, I didn't have the option of charging it to my credit card. My hair was longer back then and I curled it with electric rollers. To get by without a blow dryer, I had to wash my hair at night, let it dry while I slept, then get up the next morning and put in the curlers before I left for the day.

I tried my best to convince Robert the hairdryer was not a luxury but a necessity and we should use grocery money to procure it pronto. He responded by suggesting we pray about it, which we did. That afternoon a friend of ours dropped by and left a package on our porch. Of course, it turned out to be a blow dryer.

How random is that? Why would anybody have a spontaneous urge to give away a hairdryer? When I asked the friend what prompted her to do it, she said, "God told us you might need it."

Some might consider it a very small miracle but it touched my heart in a massive way. I needed to know that God doesn't just see Robert's needs, He sees mine too. And He doesn't just take care of what's commonly considered to be important. He's so tender and sweet, He cares about the details. He numbers the hairs on my head and even helps me style them.

During that strict budgeting season, Robert was meticulous about getting instructions from the Lord about how much we should spend on our purchases. One time we wanted a stereo stand and, after we prayed about it, Robert felt $50 was the most we should pay. We shopped the entire day and the stand we liked best was $59. I wanted to beg Robert to compromise and spend the extra nine dollars, but I knew he wouldn't do it. He was committed to obeying God with our finances. It was a matter of principle with him.

So we bought the $50 stand. Sure enough, it worked out just fine.

Over the years, things have changed. God has entrusted us with more money than we could have imagined back then. But we must still remain disciplined and obedient, so we're grateful for those early lessons. They've served us well. They've helped us learn that whether we have a little or a lot, we must look to the Lord to show us what to do with all of our resources and be faithful to obey.

I'm sure every marriage is unique, but in ours, Robert keeps total track of the finances. I don't know much about them, not because he tries to hide things from me, but because I have complete trust in his stewardship and God's ability to provide for us. Thus, when Robert and I are discussing our giving, I don't have much of a reference point. I'm not sure whether an extravagant gift would be $100 or $1,000 because I don't keep the books.

Even so, we each play our part. When we're discerning what to give, Robert usually hears an amount from the Lord. I, on the other hand, operate by peace. Sometimes, he's suggested an amount and I've answered, "I have peace, if you are sure." Other times I've said, "I don't know much about our finances, but I was hoping we could give more." There have even been times I've said, "Are you crazy?! Money doesn't grow on trees!"

It's rare, though, for me to be anything less than excited about giving. Both Robert and I have grown to love it. Giving has become part of our nature. Sometimes we try to stop ourselves, but mostly we egg each other on like we did recently when we were about to give a man $100 to meet a small need. We were driving away from the ATM with the cash in hand and we started talking about it. Within a few minutes, we'd agreed $100 wasn't enough so we wrote a check for a much larger amount.

We were so thrilled to be able to give more. We were like a couple of kids at Christmas.

LEARNING A LESSON FROM NAAMAN

If your husband doesn't have a revelation of the importance of putting God first in your family's finances, you may be wondering right now how all this applies to you. You may be thinking, *I want to honor the Lord by tithing and giving. I want to enjoy the blessings that come with putting first things first in our family finances. But my husband gets upset every time I bring it up. What can I do?*

I hear that question a lot, and here's what I usually recommend.

First, follow Esther's example by making an appeal. When you sense the time is right and you have an open door from the Lord, share with your husband what's in your heart about tithing and giving. In a gracious, submissive way, present your perspective and make your request. If he responds negatively, don't pressure or condemn him. Accept and honor his decision. Then just keep praying for him and expecting God to move on his heart.

Second, if you have some funds that are yours to do with as you please, practice tithing with those. Then watch for ways God is blessing you and share them with your husband. Let him see how tithing and giving is working in your life.

Finally, trust the Lord to understand your situation and extend mercy to you as you submit to the authority structure He has ordained in your home. Take comfort in the story of Naaman. He was a Syrian military commander in the Old Testament who was healed of leprosy under the ministry of the prophet, Elisha. After his healing, he rejected the heathen gods of his homeland and declared, "Indeed, now I know that there is no God in all the earth, except in Israel" (2 Kings 5:15).

Then Naaman realized he had a problem. As a servant of Syria's king, his responsibilities included accompanying the king when he went to pay homage to the Syrian idol, Rimmon. Somehow Naaman had to reconcile his devotion to God with his obligation to submit to his king's authority. So he said to Elisha:

"YOUR SERVANT WILL NO LONGER OFFER EITHER
BURNT OFFERING OR SACRIFICE TO OTHER GODS,
BUT TO THE LORD. YET IN THIS THING MAY THE
LORD PARDON YOUR SERVANT: WHEN MY MASTER
GOES INTO THE TEMPLE OF RIMMON TO WORSHIP
THERE, AND HE LEANS ON MY HAND, AND I BOW
DOWN IN THE TEMPLE OF RIMMON; WHEN I BOW
DOWN IN THE TEMPLE OF RIMMON, MAY THE LORD
PLEASE PARDON YOUR SERVANT IN THIS THING."
THEN [ELISHA] SAID TO HIM, "GO IN PEACE."
(VV. 17-19)

What God did for Naaman, he will do for you. If you'll obey
Him by giving what you can while still honoring the authority of
your husband, He will bless you according to the sincerity of your
heart and you can "go in peace," knowing you have done all God
expects you to do.

MORE THAN DOLLARS AND CENTS

Although finances are a big part of putting God first, they're not
the only part. He ought to be our priority in everything. We should
esteem Him and give Him first place in our time, our actions, our
affections, our work ... in everything. If we don't put Him first in
those areas, we can't expect Him to bless them.

Time is a major issue, especially for women. We have to budget
time just like we budget money. If we don't prioritize and give God
first claim on the hours in our day, other things will eat them up.
If we do give Him the time He deserves, we'll have to say no to
things that, although they may be good-things, are not God-things.

When my kids were small, for example, I had to limit their

activities somewhat. I couldn't allow myself to be chasing soccer, softball, and baseball games all week long. Those are great sports, but they can run moms ragged. So I had to say no to some of them.

I also had to pass up invitations for neighborhood get-togethers to make time for the small discipleship groups that were an essential part of my service to the Lord. Hardest of all, I had to opt out of some activities with my friends. I couldn't be a social butterfly, always going out to lunch and shopping with my buddies, while keeping God first and managing my family at the same time.

I'm glad now, though, that I've chosen to make the Lord my priority in all the different departments of my life. Even if it required some sacrifices on occasion and some bold steps of faith, they don't compare to the blessings God has poured out in return.

Although some of those blessings can be measured in dollars and cents, most of them are priceless: We've had the privilege of walking with the Lord and serving Him in ways that have exceeded our wildest dreams. We've had the joy of watching our children grow up with a love for God and His church. We've seen them marry wonderful, godly mates. We've felt the thrill of wrapping our arms around healthy, happy grandkids.

And, after 30-plus years of marriage, Robert and I are closer and more in love than ever.

Yes, the Lord asked us, just as Elijah asked the widow, to surrender to Him the first of everything in our lives. But we're more than happy to do it because no matter how much we give Him, we keep on discovering we can never outgive our God.

LADY IN WAITING

Now Abraham was old, well advanced in age; and the LORD had blessed Abraham in all things. So Abraham said to the oldest servant of his house, who ruled over all that he had, "Please ... swear by the LORD, the God of heaven and the God of the earth, that you will not take a wife for my son from the daughters of the Canaanites, among whom I dwell; but you shall go to my country and to my family, and take a wife for my son Isaac."

GENESIS 24:1-4

THE PRINTING PRESS hadn't yet been invented so we can be sure Rebekah didn't get the idea from a women's magazine. It wasn't a tip she picked up from the girls who gathered at the water well, either. Even in 2,000 B.C. women didn't believe the fastest way to a man's heart was through his camels. And Rebekah was definitely hoping to find her way into a man's heart.

Granted, the Bible doesn't specifically say so. But I think it's safe to assume that like most girls her age, Miss Rebekah was searching for her prince charming. Dreaming of the one true love God had destined her to marry.

None of the local boys, it seems, had qualified. She'd checked them all out (in her own discreet way, I'm sure) and prayed, "Oh God, please *not* them!" Thus, with her femininity in full bloom, her biological clock ticking, and no spousal possibilities in sight, Rebekah had been left with no other option but to wait ... and wait ... and wait for Mr. Right.

Then one evening during her nightly trek to draw water from the local well, she saw the camels. Resting on their calloused, dust-caked knees, they hardly looked like the doorway to her destiny. What they looked like was work—and a lot of it. Counting the massive sand-colored heads turned in her direction, their ebony eyes trained on the freshly filled water pitcher balanced on her shoulder, Rebekah did a quick calculation. Ten thirsty camels drinking 30 gallons each, and her with a two-gallon jar equaled 150 trips from the well to the trough.

The sun slipping below the horizon marked the end of a full day's work already done. Yet, weary as she was, Rebekah couldn't help smiling at the doleful faces of her 10 ardent admirers. Too bad she hadn't found even one suitor as fascinated by her as this pack of dromedaries. It was also too bad that their apparent owner, who came running to meet her, looked as old as her father and as thirsty as the camels.

With a silent sigh, Rebekah shrugged her shoulders. She would have to wait a little longer for heaven to send her a husband. In the meantime, she would meet the need at hand. She'd take the opportunity the Lord had given her.

Turning toward the aging stranger hurrying toward her, she

heard the request she'd expected.

"Please let me drink a little water from your pitcher," he said.

Offering him the jar, she nodded her assent. "Drink, my lord," she said; and as a cranky camel snorted his complaint, she added, "I will draw water for your camels also, until they have finished drinking." Then she quickly emptied her pitcher into the trough, ran back to the well to draw water, and drew for all his camels. And the man, wondering at her, remained silent so as to know whether the LORD had made his journey prosperous or not (Genesis 24:19-21).

Rebekah had no idea during the next few hours as she perspired in the Middle Eastern heat and played hostess to a guzzling gaggle of humpbacks that with every trip to the trough she was moving one step closer to her Prince Charming. She could never have imagined that within 48 hours these same creatures who were taking advantage of her hospitality without so much as a thank you would be carrying her to the home—and the man—of her dreams.

Abraham's servant, on the other hand, grew more certain of it by the moment. As he considered Rebekah's willingness to do not only what he'd asked but even more, he felt sure this was the woman God had selected. The sweetness of her attitude as she served convinced him this gracious beauty was divinely appointed to be the wife of his master's son, Isaac—one of the most godly, prominent, and wealthy men around.

So it was, when the camels had finished drinking, that the man took a golden nose ring weighing half a shekel, and two bracelets for her wrists weighing ten shekels of gold, and said, "Whose daughter are you? Tell me, please, is there room in your father's house

FOR US TO LODGE?" SO SHE SAID TO HIM, "I AM THE
DAUGHTER OF BETHUEL, MILCAH'S SON, WHOM SHE
BORE TO NAHOR." MOREOVER SHE SAID TO HIM,
"WE HAVE BOTH STRAW AND FEED ENOUGH, AND
ROOM TO LODGE." THEN THE MAN BOWED DOWN
HIS HEAD AND WORSHIPED THE LORD. AND HE
SAID, "BLESSED BE THE LORD GOD OF MY MASTER
ABRAHAM, WHO HAS NOT FORSAKEN HIS MERCY AND
HIS TRUTH TOWARD MY MASTER. AS FOR ME, BEING
ON THE WAY, THE LORD LED ME TO THE HOUSE OF
MY MASTER'S BRETHREN." (VV. 22-27)

GOD WILL NOT PRESS FAST FORWARD

Like Rebekah, we all spend seasons of our life as ladies in waiting.
When we're single we may have to wait on a husband. When we're
married we may have to wait on a pregnancy. If we're in business,
we might wait on a promotion, a raise, or a better job opportunity.
If we're called to ministry we'll have to wait for an open door and
for the voice of the Lord to say, "Go!"

For most of us such waiting comes as a surprise. We tend to
expect our God-ordained destiny (or at least the next phase of it)
to unfold overnight. But it never happens. Not to me. Not to you.
Not to anyone. Everybody—and I mean everybody—who wants
to live out God's will for their life must learn to wait.

God isn't into instant. He has no microwaveable plans. There
are no Go-Straight-to-Your-Divine-Destiny cards shuffled into
the Master's monopoly game of life. And no matter how much we
whine, beg, or even pray, God will not press the fast forward button
and advance our story straight to the scene of our dreams.

I realize this sounds like bad news. In today's culture, nobody likes to wait. For the most part, we're in major hurry-up mode. We complain if we have to wait 20 minutes for our food at a restaurant. That may be okay when it comes to tacos and burgers, but it's a problem when dealing with God because He is absolutely famous for taking His time.

It's not because He's slow, either. When He's the only one involved, He can create a world in a week. But when He's working with human beings, He deliberately alters His pace. He includes seasons in our development where, externally anyway, it looks like we're making no ... progress ... at ... all. If we get antsy and start to put our foot on the accelerator, He simply reminds us to:

- Wait for the Lord; be strong, and let your heart take courage; wait for the Lord! (Psalm 27:14, ESV).
- Be strong, and let your heart take courage, all you who wait for the Lord! (Psalm 31:24, ESV).
- Be still before the Lord and wait patiently for him; fret not yourself ... (Psalm 37:7, ESV).
- Wait for the Lord and keep his way, and he will exalt you to inherit the land (Psalm 37:34, ESV).

Such scriptures are usually not what we want to hear. So we may try to find ways around them. Attempting to remain spiritual, we might check out the Hebrew word *qavah*, which is translated "wait" in those verses. We might dig through Bible dictionaries and concordances to see if it could possibly mean anything else.

Actually, I've already done that. I figured this chapter could be more fun if I uncovered a definition for *qavah* that would allow us to proceed full speed ahead whenever we wanted or (at the most) just slow down for a few minutes and then roar forward like a Ferrari.

But, sadly, I couldn't come up with anything like that.

According to Strong's concordance, the definition of *qavah* is unequivocal: It means to *wait*. It also means *to hope, looking eagerly for something with expectancy;* but that doesn't help us much. In fact, it adds to the challenge by confirming that to *qavah* in the fullest scriptural sense of the word, we must not only wait, we must do it with faith, grace and a good attitude.

In other words, we can't spend our waiting seasons tapping our fingers together, pacing the floor and saying, "Okay God, let's get this show on the road!" We can't *qavah* as God intended and be so me-focused that all we can think about as the days and months crawl by is what we want and when we want it—which, of course, is always right now.

That perspective will backfire on us. Instead of speeding us up, it will cause us to make mistakes and slow us down even further. If our attention is fixed on ourselves, we'll either get anxious and try to force things to happen too fast; or we'll get discouraged and apathetic and—in the name of leaving everything up to God—we'll neglect to use our time of waiting to prepare ourselves for our next season.

Rebekah made neither of those mistakes. That's what makes her a great mentor. She remained patient and expectant while she waited. She refused to get in a hurry, ditch the dream God had put in her heart, and hitch herself to one of the local yokels just because he was readily available. Yet she continued to show initiative. She kept on watering camels. Although at the time it must have seemed like an activity so mundane that in the grand scheme of things it couldn't possibly matter, it set her apart from all the other girls around her. It made her so attractive she never had to go looking for her dream—because her dream came looking for her.

A PATTERN WORTH FOLLOWING

What was it about Rebekah that was so special?

She loved to serve. In her time of waiting, she didn't concentrate on her own unfulfilled dreams but on what she could do for others. She proved that becoming a blessing to someone else positions us perfectly to be blessed ourselves.

Although it's not a principle that applies exclusively to single girls, I've seen it work for a number of them over the years—usually when they least expect it. Take Elizabeth Tooley, for example. After going through a painful divorce, she wanted to find a place to serve and decided to devote some of her time to working with the youth ministry at our church. She didn't do it to find a mate, or even a date. She just wanted to be of service. But one of the kids whose father was single and working with the youth too got an idea, and said, "Dad, you need to meet her."

He did and fell in love. So did she. Now they're happily married and serving God together.

Come to think of it, I wound up with Robert in a similar way. When I first got saved I fell so in love with God and the church, I volunteered to serve any way I could. I went to visit the elderly on visitation night. I spent my summers working in Vacation Bible School. I sang in the choir. Whatever I could do to help out in any area of ministry, I did.

So when Robert's friends told him that dating a good girl would help him get his life on a godly track, I was the obvious choice. I didn't plan it that way. Meeting a husband wasn't my motive for serving. What young husband-hunter pursues her goal by visiting elderly shut-ins? Yet doing it helped set me up for my destiny. Serving at the church landed me a lifelong date with the man of my dreams.

When I look back on my life, I see over and over how serving has opened the door to good things for me. It's still happening today. I'm a servant now as much as I've ever been; and as I continue to serve, my destiny keeps unfolding.

Study the Bible and you'll see the pattern:

- Saul was serving his father by searching for lost donkeys when he bumped into the prophet Samuel and ended up anointed to be king.
- David was serving his brothers by bringing them provisions on the battlefield when he encountered Goliath.
- Deborah was serving as a prophetess when God spoke to her about conquering Sisera.
- The widow was serving Elijah when she got her needs met and her son raised from the dead.
- The woman at the well served Jesus and got a whole-life makeover.
- The disciples served Him and stepped into their destiny as the apostles of the Lamb.

Robert and I have followed the same pattern as we've walked out God's plan for our life and ministry. Although He'd put pastoring in our hearts, we had to wait seven years for Robert to be a senior pastor. While we were waiting, we served other people's visions. We worked as hard to help them succeed at what God had called them to do as we work now to fulfill our own vision. We tried our best to be faithful in the place the Lord had given us and constantly searched for ways to improve other people's lives.

As we did, the Lord trained us for the next season of our dreams. He gave us valuable insights into the work of the ministry. He opened our eyes to the dynamics of the employer-employee relationship.

We saw from the perspective of employees what leaders can do to help and to hinder those who are following them. We tucked away each lesson in our heart, purposing to remember it so that when we became leaders and employers ourselves we could be a greater blessing to the people working for us. Although Gateway isn't a perfect place and we aren't perfect employers, our staff benefits every day from what we learned in our time of waiting.

GETTING OURSELVES OFF OUR MIND

Serving not only prepares us for major aspects of our destiny, it also helps us handle the minor difficulties we encounter along the way. I renewed my acquaintance with this fact recently when Robert and I were trying to sell our house. We had a contract on it, but the potential buyers kept creating one problem after another.

First, they insisted we lower the price. "Okay," we said.

Next, they asked us to throw in some extras for free. "All right," we said.

During the inspection process, they came up with 30 changes they wanted us to make on the house. We agreed to a few just to make them happy. We had electrical work done. We filed a request with the insurance company for a new roof—even though we knew perfectly well the roof had years of life left on it. But when the buyers came back with another list of thousands of dollars worth of things they wanted done, we called it quits. After wasting a ridiculous amount of time, money, and energy, we let the deal fall through.

One night as I lay in bed resenting the situation and hoping for another contract, I decided to read my Bible until I could go to sleep. Pulling up the Bible app on my phone (so I could read in the dark), I landed on the story of Abraham and Sarah in Genesis 20. I know the passage well. It tells how King Abimelech took

Sarah, intending to add her to his concubines, and how the Lord responded by striking all of his wives with barrenness. When Abimelech, realizing what he'd done, restored Sarah to Abraham safe and sound, Abraham prayed "and God healed Abimelech, his wife, and his female servants" (v. 17).

As I read the story, it hit me that Abraham and Sarah themselves were barren at the time Abraham prayed for Abimelech. Although they'd believed God for a child for years, they hadn't yet received the manifestation of their faith. Most of us would feel inadequate in such a situation. We'd be reluctant to pray for somebody else to receive something we're still lacking ourselves.

Yet Abraham did it—and God answered his prayer. Abimelech's wives started having babies again.

Immediately afterward, something else happened:

> THE LORD VISITED SARAH AS HE HAD SAID, AND THE LORD DID FOR SARAH AS HE HAD SPOKEN. FOR SARAH CONCEIVED AND BORE ABRAHAM A SON IN HIS OLD AGE, AT THE SET TIME OF WHICH GOD HAD SPOKEN TO HIM. (GENESIS 21:1-2)

As I thought about that story, I resolved to get myself and my own situation off my mind. I determined to shake off my selfishness and start praying for somebody else. Scrolling through my mental rolodex, I came up with a handful of friends with houses for sale and began to pray for them. (One of them told me later they noticed more people coming to look at their home about the time I began to pray.)

Within three days, Robert and I received a solid offer on our house from some very nice people. Dealing with them was delightful.

After we signed the contract, they waived the inspection process and the sale went through with amazing speed. The entire experience was a blessing.

I'm not suggesting this as some kind of formula. I'm not saying that by praying for others we can make God put the rush on our own order. But I do believe it's a powerful way to defeat the devil. When he's harassing us, telling us God has forgotten us, that He's playing a cruel trick on us by making us wait, we can get the upper hand by becoming a blessing to somebody else. We can open the way for God to make vital changes in our hearts and help us become less selfish and more loving.

I'm convinced the Lord can do a lot more, both in us and for us, when we're not so self-absorbed that all we can think about is me, me, me. I also believe He gets more pleasure out of giving to us when we're focused on giving to somebody else. As a parent, I know how that can be. When my children were small, I didn't enjoy being generous toward them if they were always saying, "Give me! Give me!" When they pressured and manipulated me with their demands, I tended to resent it. But my heart melted when they came to me on someone else's behalf and said, "Mom, could we do this to help my friend? He really needs it." Suddenly I not only wanted to bless their friend, I wanted to bless them too!

Don't you think our heavenly Father feels the same way?

IMPROVING YOUR SERVANT SKILLS

Although our motivation in serving should never be to draw attention to ourselves, this is a fact: a servant's heart will be recognized. People will notice us, just like Abraham's servant noticed Rebekah, when we serve with excellence and a sweet attitude. As we put others above ourselves and stop worrying about being praised and appreciated, ironically enough, that's when the praise and appreciation is sure to come.

Not from everybody, of course. And not always right away. Sometimes it takes a while. Sometimes we have to serve simply as unto the Lord for a season with no one else watching. But eventually, God will bring just the right person across our path and they'll take an interest in us.

Nobody ever reaches their destiny without the help of someone else. So, if we stay on track with God and keep serving, we can count on it: Somebody is going to recognize our potential. Someone is going to believe in us and recommend us. Someone is going to be impressed with how graciously we water their camels. When they do, we'll be on the way to our next season.

In the meantime, it just makes sense to improve our servant skills. So here are five suggestions that will help.

1. Look for practical ways to improve another person's life. Don't try to impress anybody with your great gifts and abilities, just do what needs to be done. That's what Debra Leckie did. She was hired as a temp at Synopsys to answer the phone. After a few days, she saw she wasn't staying busy, so she offered to file and prepare documents between phone calls. Before long she was the office manager. The same thing happened with Jan Greenwood. She started out in our office as an intern. She saw needs, began meeting them, and before long she was a pastor in the women's ministry.

2. Guard your heart. When you serve someone you often see what no one else can see. (The lady who cleans my house can tell you my dirtiest secrets! She knows better than anyone else the truth about how I manage my home.) Getting those glimpses of other people's imperfections can tempt

you to become disappointed and disillusioned. But don't give in to the temptation. Just pray for people and let God be the judge. There may also be times when you feel others are taking advantage of you. When that happens, keep your eyes on Jesus. Remind yourself you're serving Him and it will be okay. The people Jesus served took advantage of Him too—yet God rewarded Him for His faithfulness in the end. He'll do the same for you.

3. Serve with joy and be patient. Joshua served Moses for 40 years without grumbling or complaining. He had a promise from God about taking the Promised Land but he had to wait a long time to see it fulfilled. His joyful, patient service prepared him for his destiny. Yours will prepare you too.

4. Do more than you're asked and do it before you talk yourself out of it. Jesus said, "Whoever compels you to go one mile, go with him two" (Matthew 5:41). Real servant-minded people do something extra. They do something unexpected, not because they want to be recognized but because they want to be a blessing. The year my son, Josh, and daughter-in-law, Hannah, lived with us, Hannah was always watching for ways to serve me. She would fold our clothes, cook a meal, or run an errand without my ever mentioning it to her. I tried to serve her too, but it was hard to keep up. Needless to say, I was sad when they packed up and moved out.

5. Whatever you do, do it to the best of your ability. Serve with excellence, but don't be a perfectionist. (Nothing on earth is ever perfect.) Remember you are God's ambassador, representing Him at home, at work, at church, at the grocery store, and everywhere else you go. So don't do anything half-heartedly. Give every act of service your all,

looking forward to the day when the waiting is over and you hear the Master say, "Well done, good and faithful servant!"

CHAPTER 11

A DIVINE APPOINTMENT

"But the hour is coming, and now is, when the true worshipers will worship the Father in spirit and truth; for the Father is seeking such to worship Him. God is Spirit, and those who worship Him must worship in spirit and truth."

JOHN 4:23-24

I DON'T KNOW WHO FIRST came up with the idea that it's a man's world. But I can guarantee this: it certainly wasn't Jesus. If He had that attitude, He never would have showed up in Samaria at the well of Sychar.

It was, after all, an unlikely place for a Jewish man to be. Located in a region populated by half-breed Hebrews who'd intermarried with Gentiles, Sychar's waters were anathema to pure-blooded Israelites. They'd rather faint from thirst than take a single racially contaminated sip.

Not that any of them would ever be faced with such a dilemma.

On principles of prejudice, the Jews in Jesus' day avoided Samaria altogether. If they had to travel between Judea and Galilee, they skirted around it, taking the long way through Jericho and the Jordan River. Better to walk a few extra miles than to risk rubbing elbows with a Samaritan. At least, such was the common perspective.

But, of course, Jesus was anything but common. He went to Samaria whenever He wanted. And on at least one occasion, He went there not just because He happened to be passing by but because—in the midst of a culture that believed God only speaks to and works through men—He had a divine appointment. With a woman.

A *Samaritan* woman.

She wasn't just an average Samaritan, either. She was an outcast among outcasts. A divorcee five times over with a live-in boyfriend. A social reject who'd been so ostracized by the other women in her community, she went to the well at noon rather than at sunset so she could draw water when nobody else was around.

Although I'm convinced His encounter with the woman was orchestrated in advance by God, Jesus didn't say anything about it to His disciples. He didn't tell them His Father was sending Him to minister to one lonely, hurting lady who desperately needed a life-changing interaction with Him. He just made it clear that on His way from Judea to Galilee, "He needed to go through Samaria."

So He came to a city ... called Sychar, near the plot of ground that Jacob gave to his son Joseph. Now Jacob's well was there. Jesus therefore, being wearied from His journey, sat thus by the well. It was about the sixth hour. A woman of Samaria came to draw water. Jesus

SAID TO HER, "GIVE ME A DRINK." FOR HIS DIS-
CIPLES HAD GONE AWAY INTO THE CITY TO BUY FOOD.
(JOHN 4:4-8)

As I've said before, throughout the Bible God treats women with special tenderness. So it's no wonder that Jesus' first few moments with the Samaritan woman were gentle and sweet. He didn't belittle or berate her for the mess she'd made of her life. He didn't look down His nose at her or even preach to her. Instead, He revealed to her His humanity. Dusty and tired, He simply asked her for some water.

It may not sound like much to us, but from the Samaritan woman's perspective, the request was monumental. Most likely, she'd never been spoken to by a Jewish man. Because her race and gender made her unacceptable, she expected Jesus to either ignore or despise her—in silence. Yet He spoke to her. He not only acknowledged her existence, He approached her as if she had value, as if she had something to give.

Even if it was only a cup of water.

Turning to look at Him, she must have paused for a moment to study His kindly face and sort out her confusion before she asked:

"HOW IS IT THAT YOU, BEING A JEW, ASK A DRINK
FROM ME, A SAMARITAN WOMAN?" FOR JEWS HAVE NO
DEALINGS WITH SAMARITANS. JESUS ANSWERED AND
SAID TO HER, "IF YOU KNEW THE GIFT OF GOD, AND
WHO IT IS WHO SAYS TO YOU, 'GIVE ME A DRINK,'
YOU WOULD HAVE ASKED HIM, AND HE WOULD HAVE
GIVEN YOU LIVING WATER ... WHOEVER DRINKS OF
THIS WATER WILL THIRST AGAIN, BUT WHOEVER

DRINKS OF THE WATER THAT I SHALL GIVE HIM WILL
NEVER THIRST. BUT THE WATER THAT I SHALL GIVE
HIM WILL BECOME IN HIM A FOUNTAIN OF WATER
SPRINGING UP INTO EVERLASTING LIFE." THE WOMAN
SAID TO HIM, "SIR, GIVE ME THIS WATER, THAT I
MAY NOT THIRST, NOR COME HERE TO DRAW."
(VV. 9-10, 13-15)

CONFESSIONS OF "MOTHER THERESA"

Robert likes to say he married "Mother Theresa" because I got saved as a child before I had time to do anything particularly raucous. But I don't really identify much with Mother Theresa. Who I identify with is the woman at the well. Granted, I wasn't a divorcee when Jesus saved me. I had no sordid past. I wasn't what anyone would consider a shady lady. Yet I was an outcast nonetheless. As a fifth grader, my inability to read had made feel unacceptable and ashamed.

And Jesus knew it. He understood my pain just like He did the Samaritan woman's. So, just as surely as He orchestrated a meeting with her at Sychar, He set up a divine appointment with me at a Baptist church in east Texas.

My grandmother—a godly, church-planting woman—was the one who prepared me for the encounter. Several years before I got saved, I went to visit her and she tried to introduce me to Jesus by insisting I watch Billy Graham on her television set. Although I was too shy to protest, I wasn't really interested in Jesus *or* Reverend Graham at the time. I just wanted to go outside and play with my cousins. But my grandmother had made up her mind. Positioning me in front of the TV, she instructed me to "play church" by sitting still and listening to the sermon. I obeyed with the expectation that when the broadcast was over I could go outside.

But my expectation turned out to be wrong. Billy Graham happened to be preaching on all three channels at Grandma's house that night. The programs aired 30 minutes apart. I had to watch every one.

Afterward, my grandmother set me on her lap and asked me if I wanted to pray the sinner's prayer. "No, I don't," I told her. "I want to go outside and play." Then I wriggled free and dashed out the door.

Some months later, my grandmother passed away. Her departure had a great impact on me. It ignited within my heart a desire to know the Lord in the same way she had known Him. On Sundays when my parents took me to church, I started paying closer attention to the message. During the annual church revival I listened carefully to the visiting preacher. He sounded to me a lot like my grandmother, so I gave my life to Christ.

Even though I was only ten years old, encountering Jesus in a personal way as my Lord and Savior changed my course. It transformed me from an unacceptable outcast into a daughter of God, accepted in the Beloved. It opened up a spiritual wellspring inside me and helped me understand what Jesus meant when He told the Samaritan woman, "The water that I shall give will become a fountain of water springing up into everlasting life."

I must admit, however, it took me years to comprehend what Jesus said next. Although I read it many times, it made little sense to me. I had no real revelation of what He meant when He talked at the well of Sychar about the subject of worship.

Apparently the Samaritan lady didn't either. She thought that, like real estate, worship was all about location. She believed Mount Gerizim—the place in Samaria where Abraham offered Isaac and the blessings were pronounced on the early Israelites—was the right spot. But she had an inward longing to approach God properly and she wanted to be sure she was correct. So once she realized Jesus was a prophet, she said:

> "Our fathers worshiped on this mountain, and you Jews say that in Jerusalem is the place where one ought to worship." Jesus said to her, "Woman, believe Me, the hour is coming when you will neither on this mountain, nor in Jerusalem, worship the Father. You worship what you do not know; we know what we worship, for salvation is of the Jews. But the hour is coming, and now is, when the true worshipers will worship the Father in spirit and truth; for the Father is seeking such to worship Him. God is Spirit, and those who worship Him must worship in spirit and truth."
> (John 4:20-24)

WHAT'S SO IMPORTANT ABOUT WORSHIP?

I'm extremely grateful for my spiritual heritage. I learned many wonderful truths in the church I attended when I was growing up. But how to worship in spirit and truth was not one of them.

Left to formulate my own theory about it, I decided worship was a kind of nebulous, religious attitude that came in handy when you needed to get something from God. It seemed to be associated with singing—but, for the life of me, I couldn't figure out why.

The singing we did at my church seemed to be little more than filler. It helped keep the congregation occupied while the latecomers drifted in and found their places in the pews. It also gave us a chance to stand up and stretch our legs before the preaching began. But the songs didn't mean anything to us. Singing them was just a ritual.

What's worse, it was boring. Our repertoire was limited to about twelve songs. Singing three each week, we cycled through them on a monthly rotation. Every Sunday it was the same routine repeated over and over again. Nobody ever gave us a Biblical explanation for what we were doing. Nobody ever encouraged us to turn our attention toward the Lord as we sang. On occasion, the music minister would give some historical background about a particular hymn. But it didn't help much. The entire ordeal remained consistently lifeless.

It's not that we didn't have talented musicians. We did. But, even so, the need for them was lost on me. Their portion of the church service seemed like a waste of time. I couldn't connect with it. Prayer, I understood; it was talking to God. Preaching, I appreciated; it was learning about God. Singing, I didn't get. Even though the words of the songs were centered around God, they didn't teach me anything and they weren't an expression of my heart.

So what was the purpose?

It was a question I asked myself for more than a decade. Then a few years after marrying Robert, I discovered the answer one Sunday morning in the last place I expected to find it—at a charismatic church. Some friends of ours had been attending the church and were excited about it, so they'd invited Robert and me to go with them. Although we didn't normally frequent such churches, we'd been experiencing a sort of spiritual revolution in our lives. God had been opening our eyes to new revelations in Scripture. So we agreed to give the church a try.

I must confess though, we went with a critical attitude. We thought we'd see what was wrong there so we could tell our friends. But what we found was so right it startled us.

We got our first surprise before we even stepped inside the sanctuary. For the first time in our lives, we saw people waiting in line to get into church. Stuffed side-by-side into the foyer like bunch of Bible-carrying sardines, they had arrived early so that when the first service ended they could rush in and get a good seat for the second service. Such a concept was utterly foreign to me. In the church of my childhood, people often loitered outside the building until the last possible moment when, dragging their feet with reluctance, they'd finally go in.

This was definitely a different kind of church!

Once the service got underway and the music started, I encountered yet another surprise: The people sang with a passion I'd never seen before. They raised their hands in worship. They wept. Before long they were even kneeling in reverence before the Lord. The only two people in the sanctuary left standing, our hands still dangling awkwardly at our sides, were Robert and me.

As unaccustomed as we were to such exuberant worship, we were captivated by it. It was pure and amazing. *This is beautiful!* I thought.

I knew such expressions of worship were scriptural because I'd read about them in the Bible. I'd seen references to lifting holy hands and bowing to the Lord, and even dancing before Him like David did. But I'd associated those things with an Old Testament culture that had long since passed away. It never occurred to me God might still appreciate such worship. Supposing He'd gotten old, I pictured Him as an ancient grandfather who didn't want to be disturbed by a lot of loud singing and shouting. I'd assumed He was grateful that most churches had toned things down.

Clearly, I'd been wrong. As I watched those believers worship, I could sense in my heart God was pleased with what they were doing. But as much as I appreciated it, I couldn't imagine I'd ever participate.

My religious traditions wouldn't let me. Neither would my pride. Masquerading as insecurity, it restrained me by reminding me of what others might think. It deprived me of the honor of worshiping my Redeemer.

But only for a while. As Robert and I returned to that church to worship again and again, God did a work in my heart. He helped me deal with my religious junk and my pride. Gradually, I started raising my hands in worship. First just a few inches, then a little higher. When I finally lifted them all the way, I felt such a spiritual release I couldn't believe I'd waited so long to surrender myself to worshiping the Lord. I thought, *Why would I not want to honor God this way?*

Over time, worshiping became such a part of me that I didn't care who saw me do it or what they thought. What mattered was that God could see me, and I wanted to be real and transparent with Him. In a sense, worship liberated me to be myself in my relationship with the Lord. It freed me to be who I am. I discovered that because I'm created to worship God in Spirit and truth, as I worship I become more and more who I was born to be.

This is true not only for me but for every believer:

In worship, God transforms us.

In worship, we hear His voice.

In worship, we see the truths He wants to show us.

In worship, we are changed.

STOP, LOOK, AND LISTEN

"But Debbie," somebody might say, "I'm just a naturally quiet person. I'm not comfortable with demonstrative expressions of my love for God. Are they really necessary?"

Yes, they are and here's why: one-way relationships don't work.

They don't thrive and grow. For relationships to be healthy there must be a two-way exchange. Both parties must communicate what's in their hearts. That's why God instilled in us a craving to express our devotion to Him through worship. It deepens our relationship with Him in a way nothing else can.

Although worshiping corporately with other believers might initially feel awkward to those of us who tend to be more reserved and shy, it's important to our spiritual development. When Christians worship together, we stir one another's spirits. We each release rivers of living water from within us; and together, we create a flood of God's presence that opens the way to very special encounters with the Lord.

Private times of worship are precious too. One of the most powerful experiences I've ever had with God happened when I was worshiping Him all by myself. Alone in a time of prayer and praise, I had a vision. I saw myself in the Holy of Holies. It was an astonishing sight! Light so totally enveloped me that as I looked around I realized I didn't cast a shadow in any direction.

Standing illuminated and transparent before God's throne, I knew He could see through all of me. Nothing was hidden from His sight. In the Old Testament, the priests could die if they entered the holy place with their imperfections uncovered; yet I found myself able to stand without fear in the very presence of God!

As I pondered what the Lord was showing me, I saw the magnitude of His love for me. I grasped how blessed I am that God gave His Son and made the way for me to enter the Holy of Holies, filled with His righteousness and cleansed from all sin!

The information wasn't new to me, of course. I'd known it to some degree for years. But in that moment it impacted me in a deeper way. Something shifted in my heart and I was never the same again.

All because I spent time in worship. Not the lifeless kind of worship I experienced singing in church as a child, but the spirit and truth kind that comes from focusing on God.

As Robert says, true worship always begins with focus. It starts when we do what Moses did one day on the back side of the desert: He noticed a burning bush and instead of just glancing at it and passing on by, he said, "I will now turn aside and see this great sight" (Exodus 3:3). He stopped what he was doing and took time to "behold" it (v. 2).

To *behold* means to stare with a prolonged gaze, to give your full attention to something. That's what we do when we worship the Lord. We turn our attention away from everything else and concentrate on Him. Shutting out the distractions of life, we gaze at Him with the eyes of our heart. And "beholding as in a mirror the glory of the Lord" we are "transformed into the same image from glory to glory, just as by the Spirit of the Lord" (2 Corinthians 3:18).

It's a simple process, but it isn't necessarily easy. Many of us in today's fast-paced culture have the attention span of a humming bird. Our thoughts flit constantly from one thing to another. Add in the devil's attempts to distract us, and focusing on God can be a real challenge. We raise our hands in worship and wind up thinking about a deadline at work or making a mental note of what we need to pick up at the grocery store on the way home from church.

When we give in to such distractions, we miss out on one of the greatest benefits God offers us. We become ADD worshipers and rob ourselves of the blessing Moses experienced. Look back at his story and you'll see what I mean.

WHEN THE LORD SAW THAT HE TURNED ASIDE TO
LOOK, GOD CALLED TO HIM FROM THE MIDST OF

THE BUSH AND SAID, "MOSES, MOSES!" AND HE SAID, "HERE I AM." (EXODUS 3:4)

Moses heard the voice of God! Because he took time to look at the Lord, he got the opportunity to listen to Him as well.

Let me ask you a question. Have you been wanting to hear from God about something in your life and wondering why He's been silent?

Maybe He's waiting for you to turn aside and look at Him before He speaks. Maybe He's telling you through His silence what I used to tell my children when they were younger. If I wanted to make sure they heard me, I'd say, "Stop what you're doing and look at me!"

I say the same thing to Robert sometimes. He can only focus on one thing at a time. So when I want to get a message across to him in a way that truly registers on him, I ask him to *behold* me when I deliver it. I did it just recently when I was going to be away from home for a few days for a women's retreat. Because I wanted our houseplants to survive my absence, I said, "Robert, look at me. Water the plants while I'm gone."

Some believers think that since God is always with us, we don't really need to set aside time to "look" at Him. But the fact is, we do. For our relationship with God to flourish, we need to stop, look, and listen to Him. We need to come before His presence with singing (Psalm 100:2). We need to enter the Holy of Holies by the blood of Jesus and draw near to God (Hebrews 10:19-22).

Amazing things happen when we're in the presence of the Lord.

- Our enemies fall before us (Psalm 9:3).
- Mountains move (Psalm 68:8).
- We experience fullness of joy (Psalm 16:11).
- We are refreshed (Acts 3:19).

When the woman at the well came into the presence of Jesus, her entire life was transformed. She went from hiding in humiliation to heralding the Good News. She found such acceptance in Christ, she was able to reach out to a community that had rejected her for years. Having experienced firsthand the love of the Lord, "The woman left her waterpot, went her way into the city, and said to the men, 'Come, see a Man who told me all things that I ever did. Could this be the Christ?' Then they went out of the city and came to Him" (John 4:28-30).

If you're ever tempted to ask, as I did for so many years, "What's so important about worship?" think about what happened at the well of Sychar. Remember that a couple of thousand years ago, a whole city was changed because Jesus had an appointment with a solitary woman who wanted to learn how to worship.

Now He has an appointment with you.

GET UP, GET IN, GET OUT

Now it came to pass, in the days when the judges ruled, that there was a famine in the land. And a certain man of Bethlehem, Judah, went to dwell in the country of Moab, he and his wife and his two sons. The name of the man was Elimelech, the name of his wife was Naomi, and the names of his two sons were Mahlon and Chilion; Ephrathites of Bethlehem, Judah. And they went to the country of Moab and remained there.

RUTH 1:1-2

 WE KNEW WE WERE OFF TRACK when we saw the sign: *Welcome to Hugo, Oklahoma!*

With all due respect to Hugo, it was not where we wanted to be. My stomach knotting with dread, I checked the clock on the dashboard. Just a few minutes shy of my curfew! What was I going to tell my dad? Waiting for me at home in Longview (which, by the way, is in *Texas*), my father expected me to walk through the door at any moment.

How was he going to react to a call from his teenage daughter informing him that her date had gotten his directions mixed up? "No, dad, Robert and I are not just a few minutes away. We're 140 miles away ... in Oklahoma."

The laughter and conversation that had filled the car for the previous couple of hours faded to silence as Robert and I exchanged confused glances. How did we get here?

We'd spent the evening at a Christian youth event in Mount Pleasant, Texas, a town about 60 miles north of Longview. Our parents had given us permission to drive to the event alone. Although we had no idea how to get there, Robert's father had given him directions before we left.

"Take 271 North," he'd said.

It sounded simple enough, and it was. We found Mount Pleasant with no problem. When the event was over and we headed back home, Robert had followed those same directions. He'd gotten back on 271 North. We were having so much fun talking and joking, he'd driven for over two hours without noticing he was going in the wrong direction.

Robert often teases me about my blonde moments. The accidental journey to Hugo was one of his. Even though it was more than thirty years ago, I like to point to it as evidence that no matter what the color of our hair, blonde moments are an unavoidable part of being human. The question is not if we'll have them; that's a given. What varies is the degree.

Some blonde moments are silly and inconsequential. Others are serious and have significant impact on our lives. Instead of briefly diverting us to Hugo, they take us on detours that can last for decades. They divert us from our destiny and get us so far off track that we wonder if we can ever find our way back.

What should we do if we find ourselves in such a situation?

My advice is to spend some time with Naomi. She's been there. She and her husband, Elimelech, took some misguided turns that landed them not just in the wrong state but in a foreign country full of heathen gods. They made some bad choices that left Naomi as a widow, mourning in Moab for the home she'd left behind.

The couple didn't set out to make such costly mistakes, of course. They were basically good people. A descendant of Abraham, just a few rungs down the ladder from Isaac and Jacob, Elimelech hailed from a rich heritage of faith. His name even meant *God is King*. But when times got tough and his faith was tested, Elimelech lost his way.

He slipped into such an attitude of discouragement that he named his sons Mahlon and Chilion, which in Hebrew mean *sick* and *pining*. The Bible doesn't say how Naomi felt about the names but, whatever her thoughts, she went along with them. She also went along with Elimelech's ill-conceived plan to leave their hometown and go looking for greener pastures.

He came up with the idea because Bethlehem (which means *House of Bread*) had, ironically enough, run out of bread. The Israelites had fallen back into their old, rebellious habits and brought a famine on the land. Rather than living up to his name, believing that God is King and asking Him for provision and guidance, Elimelech engineered his own solution to the problem.

He packed up the wife and kids, "went to the country of Moab and remained there" (Ruth 1:2).

It wasn't necessarily a wicked plan. But it wasn't God's best, either. So as soon as they implemented it, the family started going downhill—and I mean literally *down a hill*. To reach Moab they had to descend east from Bethlehem and go by way of the Dead Sea that, at over 1300 feet below sea level, is the lowest point on the earth.

That's always the way it is. When we stop living for God and making Him our King, we're heading for the lowest part of our life. When we start trusting in ourselves instead of in the Lord, we're going down. We're on our way to our own personal Dead Sea.

It's a bad place to be, for sure. But if you ever wind up there, here's a bit of good news to encourage you: even though it's deep enough to swallow Mount Everest, no one has ever drowned in the Dead Sea. No one. The water is so filled with minerals that when people try to submerge themselves in it, they're pushed back up again.

Among the first to officially verify this fact was the villainous Roman Commander Vespasian. A ruthless man who spearheaded the destruction of Jerusalem in 70 AD, he heard rumors about the peculiar buoyancy of the sea and decided to determine their accuracy by ordering slaves to be thrown in with their hands and feet tied.

Much to the slaves' relief, the rumors turned out to be true. Instead of sinking, they floated.

You can interpret that information however you like, but I see it as a metaphor for God's mercy. Like the minerals in the Dead Sea, it always surrounds us at the lowest points in our lives. No matter how far we might descend, God doesn't want us to sink. He doesn't want us to hit bottom and drown. So His mercy is always there to lift us up and keep us afloat.

Better yet, God will even turn our lowland experiences to our advantage. He'll fuel our growth by using them the way people use the potash extracted from Dead Sea as a potent fertilizer. When we're tempted to despair because we've taken a downhill detour, this is a morsel of minutia worth considering: the encyclopedia says there's enough potash in the Dead Sea to provide fertilizer to the entire world for 2,000 years. That's a lot of growth!

DON'T JUST SIT THERE, ARISE!

Sadly, Elimelech didn't look to God when he reached his low point. He just kept on heading in the wrong direction. With his family in tow, he traveled the full forty miles from Bethlehem to Moab and settled there.

> THEN ELIMELECH, NAOMI'S HUSBAND, DIED; AND SHE WAS LEFT, AND HER TWO SONS. NOW THEY TOOK WIVES OF THE WOMEN OF MOAB: THE NAME OF THE ONE WAS ORPAH, AND THE NAME OF THE OTHER RUTH. AND THEY DWELT THERE ABOUT TEN YEARS. THEN BOTH MAHLON AND CHILION ALSO DIED; SO THE WOMAN SURVIVED HER TWO SONS AND HER HUSBAND. (RUTH 1:3-5)

Poor Naomi! It was bad enough living in a strange land outside of God's perfect plan, but doing it as a widow was even worse. In a society where women without husbands or sons to protect them were often preyed upon and neglected, Naomi was left with no family except for her two Moabite daughters-in-law. She had no way to earn a living, no security, and no future.

A lesser woman might have abandoned all hope in such a situation. But not Naomi. In her darkest hour, she caught a glimmer of the faithfulness of God. She dared to believe He would help her find her way back home. So "she arose with her daughters-in-law that she might return from the country of Moab" (v. 6).

Naomi didn't just sit around in dust and ashes. She didn't waste away the hours wishing things were different. She got up and did something. She made a commitment to change her life.

Naomi arose!

Great things can happen when God's people arise. Check it out in the Scriptures:

- "Deborah arose" (Judges 4:9) when she saw the Israelites being oppressed by Sisera, went to battle alongside Barak, and freed the nation.

- "Hannah arose" (1 Samuel 1:9) when she was barren, went to the temple to seek God for a son, and brought forth the prophet who would bring Israel back to God.

- When the prodigal son "arose and came to his father" (Luke 15:18) both the family and the fortune he had forfeited through sin were completely restored.

If something is wrong in our life, we ought to do what those people did. We should ask ourselves: In what area do I need to arise? Then we should get up and take the first step in a new direction.

The first step is everything!

For Naomi, it was a step of return, which symbolizes repentance. Reversing the direction she and her husband had taken, she turned her back on Moab. She left behind the errors of the past and the tragic graves of her loved ones. Determined to serve her God and hungry for the bread of His Word, she set her sights on her hometown.

She couldn't buy a bus ticket and be there in an hour, either. Even though Bethlehem was only forty miles away as the crow flies, to reach it she would spend days traveling through rugged terrain. She'd descend 4,000 feet—without benefit of donkey or camel—from Moab to the Arabah Valley. Then she'd climb back up 4,000 feet on the other side. With no servants, Naomi would be hauling her own luggage. Since women don't usually pack lightly and there were no roller bags back then, the trip promised to be both exhausting and excruciatingly slow.

In addition to the sheer physical challenge, other dangers lurked. Bandits hid in the giant crevices of the rocks that lined the road, attacking the most vulnerable travelers. Women traveling alone were obvious victims. They risked losing not only their possessions but their lives.

Naomi knew the chance she was taking. She'd made the trek ten years earlier. She understood full well the strain and the perils involved. So it must have taken courage for her to embark on the journey again.

The same can be true for us. Going back and finding God when we've strayed away from Him often requires courage and determination. The road can be tough. Sometimes we forget that.

In my years of ministry, I've met many women in the process of returning from their Moabs who've come down with spiritual amnesia and don't remember how they ended up there. They call the church from some barren spiritual place they reached by hiking for years in disobedience to the Lord, and they expect us to give them a helicopter ride that will get them back home in an instant.

We'd do it for them if we could, but it's seldom possible. Usually when Christians find themselves miles outside of God's will, the journey back is a process. It takes fortitude, effort, and time.

I know something about how grueling such trips can be—not necessarily because I've wandered so far off track spiritually, but because I own a bicycle. Most people don't know it but I have a touring bike. It's the type that's super light and can potentially go very fast. When it was new and I hadn't ridden it much, I took it for a spin out in the country. Pedaling up the hills and racing down I started out my ride feeling like quite the athlete—making good time and looking cool.

After riding a few miles, I encountered a particularly long ascent.

No problem. I knew just what to do. Slowing my pace, I adjusted the gears and pumped my way to the top. Then as I crested the hill, right in front of a carload of onlookers, I toppled to the ground.

There was nothing glamorous or even exciting about my fall. I just tipped over—plunk!—like a kid learning to ride without training wheels. My knee took the brunt of the crash. Bleeding and throbbing, it was almost as wounded as my pride. I felt sure it was broken. It wasn't, of course. But nonetheless, I pitied myself as if it was.

After disentangling myself from handlebars and spokes, I stood alone on the side of the road and yearned with all my heart to be home. I thought about the miles I'd ridden. I did not want to re-ride them. I wanted Robert to come get me, lift me lovingly into the car, and drive me home. So I tried to call him on my cell phone. Out there in the boonies the signal was too weak. I couldn't reach him.

There was only one thing to do: pedal my way back. With my knee mangled and screaming for the emergency room, I had to re-mount my bicycle, get back on the brutal asphalt, and ride.

In a sense, that's what we all have to do when we get off track and skin our spiritual knees. It's certainly what Naomi had to do. As she turned her face toward Bethlehem, she probably wondered, *Will anyone there be kind to me? Will my friends still care about me? Will my life there ever be good again?* And with those questions unanswered, she had to start the journey home.

MAKE AN ALL-IN COMMITMENT

Women don't like to go much of anywhere alone. Whether we're shopping, going to lunch, or just stopping by the restroom, we prefer to take a girlfriend or two with us. So it's no surprise that initially Naomi invited her daughters-in-law to join her on her trip back home.

What's surprising is the fact that, before they'd gone very far, she rescinded the invitation.

A kind and unselfish lady, Naomi began to think about what life in Bethlehem would be like for the two Moabite girls. Their people were descendants of Abraham's nephew, Lot, but they'd spent their lives worshiping heathen gods. Unfamiliar with Jewish customs and traditions, in Israel they'd feel like foreigners in a strange place. They'd feel like Naomi felt while living in Moab.

I'm asking them to do something I'm unwilling to do myself, she thought. *I'm asking them to live like outsiders, to worship another God.*

As much as Naomi desired the companionship of her daughters-in-law, she wanted even more to do what was best for them. So, encouraging them to go back home, she said:

"Go, RETURN EACH TO HER MOTHER'S HOUSE. THE LORD DEAL KINDLY WITH YOU, AS YOU HAVE DEALT WITH THE DEAD AND WITH ME. THE LORD GRANT THAT YOU MAY FIND REST, EACH IN THE HOUSE OF HER HUSBAND." SO SHE KISSED THEM, AND THEY LIFTED UP THEIR VOICES AND WEPT. AND THEY SAID TO HER, "SURELY WE WILL RETURN WITH YOU TO YOUR PEOPLE." BUT NAOMI SAID, "TURN BACK, MY DAUGHTERS; WHY WILL YOU GO WITH ME? ARE THERE STILL SONS IN MY WOMB, THAT THEY MAY BE YOUR HUSBANDS? TURN BACK, MY DAUGHTERS, GO; FOR I AM TOO OLD TO HAVE A HUSBAND. IF I SHOULD SAY I HAVE HOPE, IF I SHOULD HAVE A HUSBAND TONIGHT AND SHOULD ALSO BEAR SONS, WOULD YOU WAIT FOR THEM TILL THEY WERE GROWN? WOULD YOU RESTRAIN YOURSELVES FROM HAVING HUSBANDS?

No, my daughters; for it grieves me very much
for your sakes that the hand of the LORD
has gone out against me!" (RUTH 1:8-13)

One of the girls, Orpah, yielded to Naomi's pleas. She tearfully kissed her mother-in-law goodbye and went back to her family in Moab. In doing so, she followed the example of one of her ancestors, Lot's wife. Do you remember her story? She and Lot lived in Sodom in the days just before the fire and brimstone fell. When God sent angels to help their family escape the destruction, she went with them and fled the city. But before they reached their God-ordained destination, she changed her mind. She looked back toward Sodom and turned into a pillar of salt.

I think Orpah suffered a similar fate. Because she glimpsed the way of the Lord and yet chose not to follow it, her heart became hardened. She spent the rest of her life with the heathen ... and without God.

Naomi's other daughter-in-law, Ruth, did just the opposite. She made the choice we all have to make if we want to find our way back to the center of God's will: She got in! Refusing Naomi's repeated appeals for her to return to Moab, she made one of the most eloquent speeches in the Bible:

"Do not urge me to leave you or to return
from following you. For where you go I will
go, and where you lodge I will lodge. Your
people shall be my people, and your God my
God. Where you die I will die, and there will I
be buried. May the Lord do so to me and more
also if anything but death parts me from you."

AND WHEN NAOMI SAW THAT SHE WAS DETERMINED
TO GO WITH HER, SHE SAID NO MORE.
(VV. 16-18, ESV)

With that declaration, Ruth made five all-in commitments. She declared:

1. Where you go I will go.
2. Where you lodge I will lodge.
3. Your people shall be my people.
4. Your God will be my God.
5. Where you die I will die.

Ruth didn't make those commitments just to Naomi. She made them to the Lord. Determined to change her life, she renounced her former ways, her family, and—most vital of all—her idolatry. She gave herself 100% to the ways and the people of God.

Ruth wasn't just playing games, either. She meant everything she said. As soon as she and Naomi arrived in Bethlehem, she got involved in the community. Eager to be of service, she said to Naomi:

"PLEASE LET ME GO TO THE FIELD, AND GLEAN
HEADS OF GRAIN AFTER HIM IN WHOSE SIGHT I
MAY FIND FAVOR." AND SHE SAID TO HER, "GO,
MY DAUGHTER." THEN SHE LEFT, AND WENT AND
GLEANED IN THE FIELD AFTER THE REAPERS. AND
SHE HAPPENED TO COME TO THE PART OF THE FIELD
BELONGING TO BOAZ, WHO WAS OF THE FAMILY OF
ELIMELECH. NOW BEHOLD, BOAZ CAME FROM BETH-
LEHEM, AND SAID TO THE REAPERS, "THE LORD

BE WITH YOU!" AND THEY ANSWERED HIM, "THE
LORD BLESS YOU!" THEN BOAZ SAID TO HIS SER-
VANT WHO WAS IN CHARGE OF THE REAPERS, "WHOSE
YOUNG WOMAN IS THIS?" SO THE SERVANT WHO WAS
IN CHARGE OF THE REAPERS ANSWERED AND SAID,
"IT IS THE YOUNG MOABITE WOMAN WHO CAME
BACK WITH NAOMI FROM THE COUNTRY OF MOAB."
(RUTH 2:2-6)

Because Ruth got in and got connected, she immediately found favor in her new place. God's will for her began to unfold. His blessing started to manifest in her life. One of the wealthiest landowners in the city, a relative of Naomi's, welcomed Ruth as a gleaner in his fields. He even commanded his harvesters to protect her and prosper her by leaving extra grain for her to gather.

Getting all-in brings a lot of benefits. I've seen proof of it not only in Ruth's story but in the lives of people around me. I've watched my mom, for instance, make major all-in commitments two different times in her life. The first time, she and my father had recently retired from their jobs and moved to my dad's home town. My mom lived in that area in her youth, but she hadn't been there for years. Coming back as a virtual stranger, she jumped into the community with vigor. She joined a church, a garden club, and a reading club that had been meeting for 100 years. (I think some of the original members were still there!) She connected whole-heartedly with the people in her new home and made an investment in their lives.

Then, a couple of years ago, my mom moved again to the Southlake area. This time she had to make the leap without a husband to help her adjust. But she committed to get all-in anyway. Now she's one of the best volunteers at Gateway. At last count, she was involved in three small groups and committed to at least three or four other activities. Honestly, it's hard to keep up with her.

If you're sitting on the fringes of your church right now thinking, *I don't know if I want to be involved. I'm still checking things out;* take a tip from my mom and get in!

I realize you may not find the perfect fit right away. You might try one activity, decide it's not right for you, and move on to something else. That's okay. What's important is that you whole-heartedly commit to God and His people and keep participating until you connect.

"But I need a mentor to help me," you might say, "and I don't know who to ask."

Then don't ask anybody. That's not usually the way mentorship relationships are established anyway. Somebody asks Robert at least once a month to mentor them and he can't do it. He's too busy mentoring his staff and his kids, traveling and preparing messages. At times, people get upset because he's not more available to them. They feel like their destiny is messed up because Robert (or some other leader they admire) won't mentor them. But they're mistaken.

They need to stop fastening their hope on one individual. They need to get involved in activities with other godly people and find a place to serve. By getting in, they'll find their God-ordained connections. They'll develop relationships with people they can turn to when they have questions, and those people will become their mentors.

GET OUT AND MAKE AN INVESTMENT

Once we get up and get in, there's something else we must do to get back on God's path for our life. We must get out of our brokenness, out of our pain, and invest in somebody else.

In other words, we must once again follow in Naomi's footsteps.

When she arrived in Bethlehem, all she could see in herself was her shattered dreams, her ten wasted years, and her vanished resources. She was so disappointed and defeated that she told her friends they should no longer call her Naomi, which means *pleasant*, but Mara, which means *bitter*. "I went out full, and the LORD has brought me home again empty," she said (Ruth 1:21).

Others, however, viewed Naomi in a different light. Her daughters-in-law saw wonderful qualities in her. They were so attracted to her loving, unselfish nature that they didn't want to leave her. Even Orpah who chose to go back to Moab grieved over their parting. She and Ruth sensed their mother-in-law's compassion and support. Naomi's gracious spirit had made them tender toward one another.

I've said this before, but it's a point worth making again: We, as women of God, should have the same tenderness toward each other that Naomi, Ruth, and Orpah did. We shouldn't be cat fighting and climbing over each other to get recognition. We ought to be serving, supporting, and cheerleading for each other. It's the only way we're all going to experience God's best.

I was vividly reminded of that on a recent shopping trip. I walked into a store where everything looked fine, but the atmosphere was electric with strife. I didn't have clue what was going on but my spirit was grieved. Although I wanted to buy something, my heart was so on edge I couldn't make up my mind on what I wanted.

As I started to leave, I noticed the women who worked there were verbally clawing at each other. They were complaining and competing over sales. Because their attitude had so spoiled the atmosphere, I walked out without making a purchase. None of them benefitted from my business. Everybody lost.

Such things need never happen among God's grace-filled

women. We don't have to displace someone else to get a place ourselves. There's room on the Lord's stage for every one of us. We can root each other on to success because He has a platform of influence for us all.

What's more, we need each other! We hold keys to one another's success. Even in our most broken seasons, we can make life-changing investments in each other. No matter how down we may be, we all have something someone else needs.

Naomi, even in the midst of her own problems, had what Ruth needed to succeed in her new life in Bethlehem. She knew the customs of the Hebrew people. She understood the law of the kinsman redeemer and how Ruth could put it to work and find a husband in Boaz. Naomi had a plan. All Ruth had to do was listen to the plan and act on it. As she did:

- Naomi's life lessons became her teachers.
- Naomi's disappointments became her appointments.
- Naomi's pain was healed.

Think of it. Because one woman got out of her brokenness and poured herself into another, the story ended beautifully for them both: the kindly, well-respected Boaz redeemed them in every way. Foreshadowing the redemption that would one day come to all mankind through Jesus, he restored Elimelech's lost property to Naomi. He married Ruth.

> AND WHEN HE WENT IN TO HER, THE LORD GAVE
> HER CONCEPTION, AND SHE BORE A SON. THEN THE
> WOMEN SAID TO NAOMI, "BLESSED BE THE LORD,
> WHO HAS NOT LEFT YOU THIS DAY WITHOUT A CLOSE

RELATIVE; AND MAY HIS NAME BE FAMOUS IN ISRAEL!
AND MAY HE BE TO YOU A RESTORER OF LIFE AND A
NOURISHER OF YOUR OLD AGE; FOR YOUR DAUGHTER-
IN-LAW, WHO LOVES YOU, WHO IS BETTER TO YOU
THAN SEVEN SONS, HAS BORNE HIM." THEN NAOMI
TOOK THE CHILD AND LAID HIM ON HER BOSOM,
AND BECAME A NURSE TO HIM. ALSO THE NEIGHBOR
WOMEN GAVE HIM A NAME, SAYING, "THERE IS A SON
BORN TO NAOMI." AND THEY CALLED HIS NAME
OBED. HE IS THE FATHER OF JESSE, THE FATHER OF
DAVID. (RUTH 4:13-17)

A storybook ending. It's what God had in mind for Naomi and
Ruth all along. It was in *His* plan for them right from the beginning, all the way back in Moab. But they couldn't have walked it
out alone. They needed to be together. They needed each other to
accomplish God's redemptive purpose.

Isn't it comforting to know that even if we've veered off track
God still has a purpose for our lives? Isn't it thrilling to think that
whether we find ourselves in Hugo, Moab, or the Dead Sea, God
can always help us find our way back into His perfect plan?

He did it for Naomi and Ruth in a big way. He not only steered
them back on track, by giving them a great, great grandson named
King David, He wove them for eternity into the lineage of Jesus.

God will do something just as amazing for us. If we'll get up,
get in, and get out, He'll empower us to change our own lives and
bless somebody else's. He'll give us a story with a wonderful ending
and make our lives eternal testimonies to His redemptive grace.

Whether you relate to Naomi, Ruth, Rebecca, Hagar, Mary,
Eve, the widow or the woman at the well, God has a wonderful

plan for your life. Let's learn from these ordinary women that God chose to highlight their victories and struggles in His eternal Word so that we too can be blessed women.

ADDITIONAL RESOURCES FROM
PASTOR DEBBIE MORRIS

BE STILL
Exploring the Power of Rest

FEAR NOT
Overcoming Fear

GRACED
Becoming a Woman Who Lives in Grace

I AM PINK
Exploring the Value of Being a Woman

MARRIED
Foundations for Healthy Marriage

TAKE YOUR PLACE
Overcoming Insecurity

These CDs and other resources have been created to help women become all God has planned for them to be, and are available at Passages Bookstore or online at *passages.gatewaypeople.com.*

SMALL GROUP STUDY
AND LEADER'S GUIDE

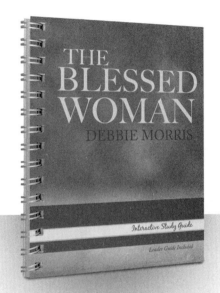

"In many ways, this is a fabulous time to be female. But it's also a complicated time. In fact, without God's guidance, it can get downright confusing."

How do you feel about being female in today's world? Do you feel thankful? Frustrated? Overlooked? Cherished? This curriculum was created to show you what the Lord wants you to know about femininity, and why He created you to be female. It is a guide to help you invite the Holy Spirit to become your mentor and guide, and to show you the sweetness of the Lord's heart for you. You will be encouraged to surround yourself with godly women who will walk alongside you, as you grow and learn to become a support to others. This guide was designed to help you pray and learn deeper "grace lessons" as you conceive, carry, deliver and nurture God's dreams and purpose for your life. *Leader's guide included.*

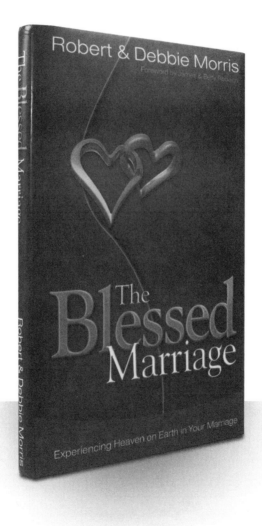

STUDIO G

The magazine title, *Studio G*, was inspired by Psalm 144:12, which is a prayer asking God "that our daughters may be as pillars, sculptured in palace style." The name reminds us that we, as Christian women, are in God's studio as unfinished works of art. Studio G is committed to reminding us of the ways of the Master Sculptor as He continues to fashion us into "women of palace style." In His studio, we discover who we are created to be and we come to realize our true worth.

SIGN UP TO RECEIVE STUDIO G:
studiogmag.com/subscribe

Find the latest edition and stay up-to-date on the latest Studio G news.

IT'S A WHOLE NEW WAY TO ENJOY STUDIO G...
visit *studiogmag.com* today!

SHARE YOUR THOUGHTS
WITH THE AUTHOR

YOUR COMMENTS WILL BE FORWARDED TO
DEBBIE WHEN YOU SEND THEM TO:

pink.gatewaypeople.com

Or

The Blessed Woman c/o
Pink Gateway Women
500 S. Nolen, Suite 300
Southlake, TX 75022

YOU CAN STAY IN TOUCH WITH DEBBIE:

TWITTER:

@psdebbiemorris

WEB:

debbiemorris.gatewaypeople.com

WEB:

theblessedwoman.org

PINK

pink
gatewaywomen

"We're committed to passing along timeless truths, not in old fashioned ways that resemble a grandmother's tea club, but in ways that relate to today's generation. We've set our sights on celebrating who we are as Christian women and connecting with one another in love. We want to share with each other what we've learned, become cheerleaders for those following in our footsteps, and reach out to receive help and instruction from those who are a few steps ahead."

Debbie Morris
The Blessed Woman

PINK

FOR MORE INFORMATION ABOUT THE MINISTRIES
OF PINK PLEASE VISIT:

pink.gatewaypeople.com

pinkimpact.com

studiogmag.com

pinkgroups.gatewaypeople.com

facebook.com/gatewaypink

twitter.com/gatewayPink

(podcast)